The Adventures of Bindi Girl

Diving Deep Into the Heart of India

Erin Reese

Published by
TRAVEL AND SOUL MEDIA
www.travelandsoulmedia.com

ISBN: 978-0-615-54766-4

Design by Red Letter Day Graphic Design (New York, NY)
Front cover photo of Bindi Girl at
Burning Man by Mona
Back cover photo of Bindi Girl on
The Andaman Islands by Jan Turnovec

Praise for The Adventures of Bindi Girl

"Lovely, lyrical, gentle, and informative. It made my world bigger."

~ **James Fadiman, author of**
The Psychedelic Explorer's Guide* and editor of *Essential Sufism

"Erin goes places, physically and metaphorically, few travelers dare to go. Her stories amuse, outrage, inspire and provoke. This isn't the tale of someone who received a book advance jetting off business class for a few weeks in an ashram. This is third class train, steerage class ship, with a dash of indulgence thrown in. Erin is a gifted, special writer, and she's the real deal as a traveler."

~ **Lynn Braz, editor and travel writer**
featured in *The Dallas Morning News*

"It's like *Eat, Pray, Love* — with teeth."

~ **Jessica Shepherd, author of *A Love Alchemist's Notebook***

"Reese reports on an India few outsiders get to witness — not the Goa parties or tourist sites or political turmoil, no. Instead she dives into the throbbing spiritual centre of India and tries to place her California soul amongst the gurus, mystics and visionaries that remain a constant of Indian religion. Yet Reese is no New Age tourist full of cosmic waffle. Her writing is both beautifully descriptive and very funny. She captures the sweaty heat of India, its madness and charm. Her own spiritual quest mixes with her lusts and frustrations to create a new kind of travel writing. If I ever return to India it will be with Bindi Girl as my guide."

~ **Garth Cartwright,**
author of *Princes Amongst Men: Journeys with Gypsy Musicians* and
More Miles than Money: Journeys through American Music

Praise for The Adventures of Bindi Girl

"Erin Reese 'gets' the spirit of India. In reading her adventures, I could almost hear the crowds and smell the curry. But more than that, I felt blessed by the soulfulness of half-a-dozen millennia. Erin was born to be in India — and to write this book."

~ **Victoria Moran, author of**
Creating a Charmed Life **and** *Shelter for the Spirit*

"Respectfully, if you want a real tale of travels in India, forget *Eat, Pray, Love*. *The Adventures of Bindi Girl* is the real thing. Reese's nitty-gritty India travelogue shows an intense, all-or-nothing commitment to a life-long spiritual path. At times tempting the reader to dive into Ma India for oneself, at times letting us live vicariously through the filth while keeping our own paws clean, this memoir shows vulnerability, respect, and gumption. Erin travels with a sense of humor and a sense of metaphor. And a sense that there is deep mystery 'neath the maya, the illusion of this material world. A must-read for any would-be traveler. 'Jai Ma!'"

~ **Alicia Dattner, comedian,** *Eat, Pray, Laugh!*

"'Milk-coming-out-of-your-nose' hilarious at times, and heartrending naked revelation at others, Reese takes us along on her unsentimental spiritual journey through India as she fearlessly follows her heart through worlds few travelers experience. Bindi Girl is a must-read for anyone who yearns to travel within and without, and who is not afraid to be transformed in the process."

~ **Pamela Lund, author of** *Massively Networked*

This book is dedicated to
the indomitable spirit in all of us.

Contents

Acknowledgments

For their love and assistance in supporting my work and vision, I would like to acknowledge the following remarkable beings:

Words cannot express enough gratitude to the brilliant Sharon Schanzer of Red Letter Day Graphic Design. Without Sharon's talent and persistence, it is doubtful Bindi Girl would have been birthed into such a beautiful physical incarnation!

Next, I thank the readers of the original Bindi Girl blog (2002-2010) for their enthusiastic response to the travel tales that made up this book. Additionally, I wish to honor Jan Turnovec, travel partner in time, for showing up right on cue for his costarring role.

And then, teammates, helpers, and cheerleaders who contributed to this project over the years: Wendie Pecharsky, Pamela Lund, Tina Marie, Becca Costello, Emma Nirmala Batchelor, Malin Wallen, Jessica and John Shepherd, Moldover, Jill Merzon, Lynn Braz, Susan Arthur, Bo Lee, Jim Kelly, Gregg Butensky, Garth Cartwright, Chhi'méd Drölma, Gigi Hindin, Jennifer Richards, Amy Taylor Chetcuti, Carolina Brown, Vanessa Spear, Robyn Miller, Steve Henderson, Suzanne Aveihle, Denise Pulver and family, and the Reese family.

A thousand and eight pranams to my teacher, Ramesh Balsekar, for Everything and Nothing. And to all those I've unintentionally omitted and those who have helped me anonymously, thank you.

And finally, I bow my head in gratitude to Mother India, for without Her incomparable mystique there would be no Bindi to shine.

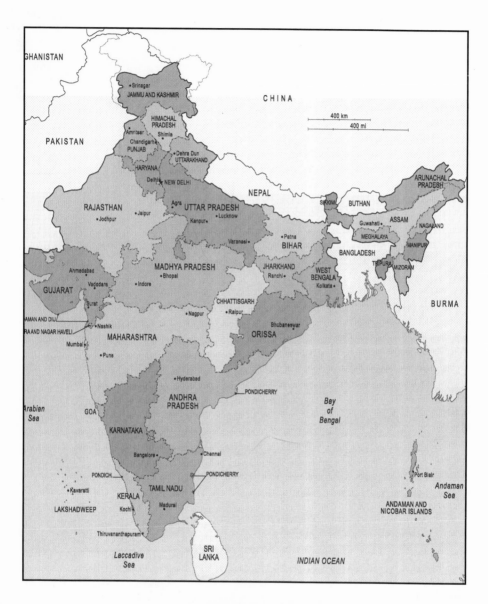

Map of India

Prologue

Hi. This is Bindi Girl.

I first appeared on the scene ten years ago when I spotted my scribe in the Black Rock Desert of Nevada. During the entire week of the Burning Man art festival, the writer Erin Reese had been plastering bindis—those glittery, self-adhesive jewels used to adorn one's third eye—on anyone who crossed her path. Never before had she enjoyed such spontaneous joy in the surprise of strangers!

Wearing some garish get-up and a big grin, Erin would tromp across the dusty desert and stick a bindi right smack-dab in the center of some unsuspecting reveler's forehead. "Now your third eye is even *more* open!" she'd proclaim.

"*W-o-o-o-o-w!*" they'd swoon, encouraging her to continue opening minds and hearts with her portable, personal mark of mysticism and fun—the simple, sparkly bindi.

When the week of bindi-fying Burning Man participants came to an end, one particular well-wisher crawled out of the dust to find her. She'd only met him for a few minutes while she was making bindi rounds, but apparently, she'd made quite an impression on this chap from Louisiana. He spotted her in the exit gate RV queue, bidding the desert adieu. He leaped out of his Winnebago and bolted after her.

She heard his shouts before she saw him—like a far-off call of the desert wild wind: "Bindi Girl! HEY, BINDI GIRL!"

Oh my God. I think that man... Yes, he means...ME! She flung open the motor home hatch to speak to him as he shuffled alongside the slow-crawling RV.

"Hi there, Bindi Girl!" he drawled, dangling off the doorstep as the vehicle trawled along. The charming blue-eyed stranger with long blond ponytail had a N'awlins twang as thick as Mississippi mud. "Can I get your email, Bindi Girl?"

This wild-eyed Southern boy had sussed out Bindi's true identity! With sparkles in her own eyes, she beamed back at him. It was the first time she had been recognized—and, appropriately named.

And that, my friends, is the origin of Bindi Girl, fearless alter ego and spunky *nom de plume* of intrepid traveler Erin Reese, who will now take us by the hand into a far-off land, diving deep into the heart of India!

PART ONE
Maiden Voyage

Erin's Story

I needed life to STOP, so I could get off the speeding train in hot pursuit of the American Dream before it turned into an American Death.

Hitting the age of thirty, I found myself ensconced in a *grabby-greedy-gotta-have-it-all* cosmopolitan lifestyle in San Francisco—and quickly burning out from trying to keep up with the role I'd been playing, but clearly wasn't for me. Sure, I'd accomplished more than I'd ever imagined: a successful six-figure career, a vibrant and superbly busy social life, all bills paid off, and a beautiful flat with a cityscape view and a rooftop garden terrace, and, and...

And, I was too exhausted to move. I simply could not go on working myself to the bone in a career that was killing me, in a culture that emphasizes ambition, $UCCE$$ and praising the name of the Almighty—the Almighty American Dollar, that is. Every day, I'd don smoothly-tailored suits and three-inch high heels, race to the office, and—with the drive of a pit bull—produce, produce, produce. I was the top-performing corporate headhunter in a commission-only position—a job at which I was indisputably talented, but with no time or energy left to breathe, to rest, to think, to BE.

When the world as we knew it plunged to pieces on September 11, 2001 and travel was declared unsafe due to terrorism, I took an entirely different tack: since I was symbolically ready to die anyway, I opted to dive off the cliff.

Within a month after making my decision, I gave up my apartment, sold ninety percent of my household possessions, packed one bag, took the cat to my mother's, and summoned every single ounce of courage I could, for I would need it. I had nothing to lose and therefore everything to gain. Where might I land? Terrified and quivering in my flip-flops, I took off for a six-month, solo journey to wander the Indian subcontinent, with no idea what I'd find on the other side of the world.

Since childhood, She had called to me—the most mysterious, the most intimidating, the most extreme of destinations I could dream of.

Her name was, is, and shall forever be: India.

Night Flight

I'm doing my best to keep my mind distracted, munching the Indian Airlines freebies—pouches of spicy, dried lentil *dal* instead of your usual peanut packets—handed out by sari-clad stewardesses. *What an odd snack.* (Chew; crunch, crunch, crunch.)

The plane cabin is so poorly compressed that the crew is dispersing clusters of cotton balls to stuff in our ears in order to alleviate discomfort. The fuselage rattles furiously, as we bumble and bounce over Bangladesh. The turbulence is so rough, I'm wondering if we'll actually make it at all.

I start to meditate, observing the breath through my nostrils—inflow, outflow—as I've been taught. What else to do when you're about to plummet to your death, except observe?

A few babies begin to wail, heads pounding in pain. I feel sorry for them; my own brain feels like it's about to burst as we begin a daring descent into Delhi.

What's awaiting me? Is this the shape of things to come? A voice, unexpected, seems to bubble up from nowhere:

India will reveal to you
the places in your heart
that must be purified.

Arrival

Oh, that night. That crazy, crazy night.

That middle of the night when I landed at Indira Gandhi International airport, arriving in Delhi on the holiday of Diwali…

Night of Lakshmi! Night of the great light!

Crackers blasting, blowing eardrums, taxi twisting and turning through the inky black night!

Whirling through the smoke-filled air, chai wallahs and street people huddling on the side of the pothole-ridden, dingy road as the driver hurls through time and space.

Crash-landing in the capital city of India, another planet entirely— there's no place like Om! Whizzing past the "March to Independence" Gandhi Memorial toward the Main Bazaar, explosions of light and kaleidoscope as fireworks shoot through the air…

This—*this* is my personal welcome party!

"HAPPY DIWALI!!!" yells India.

"HAPPY DIWALI!!!" yells the cab driver, turning his head to speak directly to me, continuing pedal to the metal, one hand steering the wheel as we barely avoid sideswiping a bumbling bullock cart and we tear into the narrow streets of the bazaar.

"HAPPY DIWALI!!!" yells the hotel night manager, shoving a box of sweets in my face as I lug my backpack up and drop it before the front desk. My first *prasad* (food blessed by the gods), that fateful night—milk sweets made from *chana* (chickpea) gram flour and loads of *ghee* (clarified butter).

Flashes of travel guide warnings pass before my eyes: to accept the stranger's sweet offering, or decline gracefully. Like Alice contemplating her next move on the chessboard, I weigh the risks: delight, diarrhea, or drugging. *Hmmm, let me think*—but not too much! That millisecond of standing there in the lobby of the cheap hotel at 3 a.m., wondering whether to go ahead and let life "EAT ME" alive, I opt to throw caution to the wind and shove the sugary cube down the hatch.

Simultaneously scared shitless and ferociously fearless.

Mother India called, I answered, and I came.

I lived to tell about it—and to share it with you, exactly as it happened. Enjoy the ride.

Welcome Om

5ᵗʰ of November, New Delhi

I made it! I'm here in New Delhi, in Pahar Ganj Main Bazaar, after about thirty-six hours of traveling from San Francisco, including three flights and a taxi ride that made me sweat.

Wow. I feel so comfortable here. It is just great. There is so much to absorb, flooding in all at once—the food, the smells, the *shit*, the grossness, the beauty.

I haven't ever seen women shine like the Indian women do, in their saris and Punjabi (*salwar kameez*) suits. I walked into a tailor shop today, picked out some material, and had a Punjabi made for around $9.00—custom fit for me—and I pick it up tomorrow. For those who aren't familiar with these suits, they are the loose pants and long, to-the-knee tops (*kurtas*) and matching shawls (*dupattas*) that women wear in India. The women wear the long scarf draped over one shoulder or both shoulders, hanging down the back.

I feel like all my prayers have been answered thus far. I'm not holding my breath, though, and I know I need to stay alert and cautious. Of course, everyone in the Main Bazaar wants to be your friend, chatting you up and inviting you to see their wares. I don't have the slightest idea how to bargain in a friendly, non-defensive fashion yet, which is ironic considering my former career as a corporate headhunter in San Francisco.

Via the *Lonely Planet* online bulletin board, I made arrangements to meet a fellow traveler this morning at our hotel. This young man from London is also a meditator—he's on his way to Kathmandu for a long winter's retreat at a Buddhist monastery. I am *so* grateful that I made these meeting arrangements, for I would have been more than a wee bit intimidated walking alone my first hours through the Main Bazaar, which is where my little hotel is.

Today, the two of us went to the New Delhi train station and bought our onward journey rail tickets. Tomorrow night, I'm taking a Second Class sleeper to Dharamsala in the northwest corner of the nation. Dharamsala is where His Holiness the XIV Dalai Lama and the Tibetan government are living in exile. In about a week, I am scheduled to take a ten-day Introduction to Tibetan Buddhism course at a center there, so I will arrive several days early in order to adjust to the high altitude—and to decompress a bit.

Things are so incredibly inexpensive here. I really, really don't like to shop in the West. I find it bothersome and a chore. But, here—boy, oh boy, I could drop some serious cash. I find myself reeling from the colors, the materials, the pure sensory glory of it all. AND I HAVEN'T EVEN BEEN IN DELHI TWENTY-FOUR HOURS!

I walked into my slummy (by American standards) hotel last night feeling giddy and grateful to all the angels and supportive mortals who helped me make it thus far. I love my hotel; it even has a rooftop restaurant overlooking Delhi that is so peaceful and a perfect place to chill out.

The air quality here is astounding. Even in the daytime, it is slightly dark. The sun is a disk hidden behind smog so thick it looks like the moon during an overcast dusk. I don't think I'd ever want to jog here, even if I did have my running shoes. Besides, I'd never make it past the cows and shit. (There's a rumor that the prison sentence for hitting a cow and killing her, by car, is worse than hitting and killing a human. The cows are our mothers, you know.)

Oh, yes! Last night the entire country welcomed me to India! The evening I arrived was the peak of the "festival of lights," Diwali—a five-day festival welcoming the god Rama (an incarnation of the protector god, Vishnu) home from the forest. The Indians light the way for Rama to get back to his family, and the country goes mad with fireworks and firecrackers. Diwali is brighter than any Christmas light fest I've ever seen!

My connecting flight was three hours late from Bangkok, and I was a drooling, brain-dead Gumby by the time I arrived in Delhi. But when I rode in that night taxi from the airport to my hotel, I saw all the lights and joyous festivity of Diwali, and felt the welcoming spirit of all Delhiites, and I thought, wow, perfect timing. If I had arrived "on time," I would have missed the beauty of it all!

I am vibrating with a warm heart, filled with energy and joy, rolling with it all—and so grateful I took the plunge to dive into India.

From Saris to Snow Level

7th of November, McLeod Ganj

I arrived late afternoon yesterday in McLeod Ganj, near Dharamsala, in the north Indian state of Himachal Pradesh. What an absolute contrast from Delhi! I actually changed countries, in essence. All of a sudden, I've gone from being inundated with saris, sticky heat and filth, to being in Tibet.

Well, not quite Tibet. Due to the huge influx of tourist income, McLeod Ganj is totally westernized, which makes it feel like an Indian version of Aspen or Tahoe.

I have barely settled in, but I think it will take a few days to adjust to the high altitude. I checked into a guidebook-recommended Tibetan hotel, which, unsurprisingly, has turned out to be very popular with backpackers—it's a real epicenter of activity replete with Internet, a busy restaurant, and bakery.

But, it's a little too hip and hopping for my taste. I need a respite, so I'm moving my things in an hour or so to the guest house my intuition was originally hinting at, a peaceful little place off the beaten path, also run by Tibetans. I took an early morning walk over there to check it out. The views are spectacular and the place is quiet and very clean. The smell of Tibetan incense greeted me as I walked in.

The Tibetan people are as magical and hypnotizing to look at as the

Indians, but different. I lose myself in awe, staring at the people of Asia. (I suppose that is what they might be doing in return as I am ogled everywhere I go. I know much of the attention I receive is due to the fact that I am a foreign woman, traveling alone. If I were blonde, I would be looked at even more.) I see such a deep, old wisdom in the faces of the Tibetans, a life of cold mountain terrain and fierce conditions. I could stare at the elders for hours. I want to ask them about their lives, their old land, the invasion of the Chinese, their courageous acts as refugees.

In contrast, I see wisdom and ancient knowledge in the Indians, yes; but with their softer faces and big doe eyes, I see more of an innocence—almost childlike—and emotionality. Like water as opposed to the earthy Tibetans, I suppose.

Just when I finally get myself dressed in traditional clothing of Indian women (my personal-tailored *salwar kameez*), I am in a new land where the Tibetan women dress in *chupas*—long, heavy fabric dresses with colorful aprons. Their hair is piled high on their heads in braids mixed with colorful threads—beautiful.

The first thing I am grateful for in McLeod is the fresh air. I felt like smoking cigarettes in Delhi to calibrate my oxygen intake with the pollution. Here in McLeod, with crisp and clean Himalayan foothill air, the views of the Kangra Valley are spectacular. McLeod is a high hill settlement, and the residences are built precariously on steep mountainsides. Thousands of multicolored Tibetan prayer flags fly across the skies—and I can actually see the sun and the sky here (as opposed to Delhi).

I am happy, if a little confused, boggled—disoriented—by the quick switch from the full-on India of Delhi, to touristy Tibetan Dharamsala. I'm not sure which country I am in at the moment. I know the next step is to settle into a place for a while, to really feel the people and the culture.

My ten-day Tibetan Buddhism introductory course in Mahayana meditation begins next week. Until now, my meditation practice has been in the Theravadan tradition known as Vipassana, which is widely spread throughout Burma (Myanmar), Thailand, Sri Lanka, and other parts of Southeast Asia. Vipassana is a Pali word from the time of the Buddha, which means "seeing clearly." While my Vipassana sitting practice has been and continues to be invaluable, I feel I owe it to myself to become familiarized with the other "branch" of Buddhism while I am here in McLeod Ganj, or "Little Lhasa." This course could be a door-opener to understand the Tibetan people, the history, and the teachings of His Holiness the Dalai Lama—not to mention enjoying my time even more. I will be here for at least two weeks, and probably longer.

Life In "Little Lhasa"

12th of November, McLeod Ganj

Two days ago, the Dalai Lama returned from a trip to Mongolia and the entire town came out to greet him. His Holiness zipped past the well-wishers in his little car, blessing us all with his hand held up in a boon-granting pose and wearing a big compassionate smile on his face. I snapped a proper tourist photo as he drove past quite fast. I'm sure the only thing one will see in the photo will be the standard automobile. His Holiness is supposed to hold a public audience sometime later this month, but it is not for certain. He *is* one of the busiest people on the face of the planet. Even I would be unselfish enough to give the man some peace! That said, I'd still love to shake his hand and receive a blessing.

This morning I took the opportunity to visit a traditional Tibetan medical doctor. I had to bring a sample of my first urine of the morning (toted in my bag, wrapped in plastic, praying it wouldn't leak). Here's how it went:

The Tibetan doctor takes my urine container into a little side room. I watch him through the doorway as he shakes it up and observes, shakes it up and observes several times, then comes back. The doctor starts telling me things that are true right away: I have a cold (yes), and I have back problems (yes). I had an accident to my back and hips and this is still causing me much pain in my left leg (yes). He takes my pulse, gives me two "prescriptions"—funny little balls of herbs. The first series of herb balls is for the cold, and then I am to begin the second series to start healing my back and leg problem. The doctor's consultation is free. The medicine: 130 rupees, the equivalent of about US $2.25. Compare that to the cost of western medicine!

My doubts of lonely, solo traveling have been put to rest. I have met so many people here, it's "We Are the World." Actually, it suits me. I can be with a group, or another person, for a short time—a meal, a hike, or other adventure—then retire to my room or run away to a cafe to write. Even so, every time I think I'll go to a little restaurant for a cup of chai and a date with my journal, *voila!* There's the French guy I see everywhere, or the Czech girl, or the Danish couple—and I'm no longer solo. It's quite comical, actually. That's why I'm looking forward to my retreat: blessed silence.

There's a saying, "In India, you are never alone."

Monking Around

13ᵗʰ of November, McLeod Ganj

I just returned from a lovely trek with a man from Quebec and a woman from France. We hiked up the mountains to a tiny café high on a cliff, perched above a waterfall. No electricity up there—just a propane-fueled chai stand and soft drinks cooled by the fresh springs. The astonishing views made me wish I'd brought a better camera. A very sweet impression was that of the monks showing up as tiny maroon dots far below. They were hiding out from the town and the monasteries, bathing in the cold runoff from the waterfall with their undergarments on. Their beautiful burgundy robes and wraps were freshly washed and laid out on the rocks to dry in the sun; from far above, they looked like tapestries, or *thangkas*—the traditional Tibetan Buddhist mandala paintings on cloth.

I enjoy being in the presence of the monks—and here in McLeod, there are plenty! Three days ago, I went with the two Danish women to the temple complex of the Dalai Lama. I had read in the guidebook that it is sometimes possible to see the monks do their traditional debating, called "dialectics," in the courtyard.

Lucky for me and the Danes, the dialectics session was just about to begin when we got there. It's a big part of the monks' training, and such a pleasure to watch! The monks pair up and one perches on the ground while the other stands before him and begins to expound on Buddhist philosophy with fervor and flourish. When the speaking monk makes a point, he slaps his hands together in front of the other's face, very animated. I learned that they aren't "winning" based on *what* they know or how *much* they know; rather, the skill level lies in *how* they make their point.

The Tibetan secretary of the complex saw the three of us western women on the sidelines of the courtyard, standing out and relatively *very* tall—especially the two Scandinavians. We were watching the monks from a polite distance. The secretary hurried out from his office and personally escorted us directly into the middle of a good hundred burgundy-robed debaters. We could now watch close-up, seated comfortably on a bench.

This was my first exposure to the fact that no matter how "enlightened" or how monastic the monks are, they haven't entirely eliminated their egos, and they are very human. From their facial expressions and playful glances our way, it almost seemed—no, could it be? Were some of these monks actually *flirting* with us? Yes, the three of us could swear it was true.

The surreptitious courting in the courtyard was then broken. Curiosity got the better of a large Indian tourist family, so they crossed the barrier, came to our bench, and asked us what was going on. They were far more interested in us than the monks. Before we knew it, an entire family of ten, eleven—no, make that twelve!—brothers, sisters, cousins, aunties, uncles, and babies surrounded us, all clamoring to have their picture taken together. I had little kids on my lap and grandmas at my side, each family member tugging to get in the shot. And once they saw the intriguing technology of the Danish girl's digital camera, they were beside themselves. So much for the monks. We had to hightail it out of there.

It's amazing to me how the Indians have absolutely no shame gawking and staring at foreigners, especially women. On my long bus ride yesterday, there was an Indian man who blatantly stared directly into my face, less than three feet from me, for an hour straight, seemingly without blinking the entire time. I was impressed with his concentration! And his utter lack of self-consciousness. Fellow travelers say one gets used to it. I sometimes feel the urge to glance over and say, "DO YOU WANT TO TAKE A PICTURE OR SOMETHING?!" But then I just laugh and wonder to myself, is he staring because he thinks I'm beautiful or ghastly pale and alien?

Me, Myself, and Mind

1ˢᵗ of December, McLeod Ganj

I can now officially claim, "I am a Buddhist-school drop-out."

I showed up for the ten-day Mahayana course and stayed for two days. Something was not resonating with me—something about the participants, who were at varying levels of seriousness and experience, as well as the teachers, nuns, and monks. Somehow, I could not get my mind, heart, and soul around the deities, chanting, visualizations, and full regalia of the Tibetan tradition. My mind felt more cluttered than cleaned.

On Day Two, at lunchtime, I suddenly had the thought, "Wow, I could actually LEAVE!" This is a liberating concept for *moi*, as I am the type of person who usually sees things through—especially a meditation course. But, the truth was ringing in my ears; I was in the wrong place.

Perhaps, ironically, I was triggered by the reading I was doing the night before, from a book by a Rinpoche who was the actual founder of the center. In the text, Rinpoche describes the philosophy of death embraced by many Buddhists: to look each day squarely in the face and say, "This is the day I will die." If you think about it, it's true: we are simultaneously dying every moment, and being reborn every moment.

Therefore, if today is the day you are going to die, *how will you live today*?

So when I woke up in the morning on Day Three, I asked myself, if

this is the day I will die, is this place where I choose to be? Is this *exactly*
what I choose to be doing? Paradoxically, asking myself this question
catapulted me straight out of the study center that invited me to ask it in
the first place!

The timing was perfect. I happen to have dropped out of the course
just one day before a Vipassana insight meditation course was to begin
just down the road! A Vipassana course, as taught by S.N. Goenka and
assistant teachers, lasts a total of twelve days, with ten days in absolute
silence. I had completed my first such course in California last year.

I questioned myself. *Am I really ready to sit for eleven hours a day—no
speaking, no journal writing, no reading, and no food after eleven a.m.
(except lemon water), making a complete dissection of my consciousness?*
I suppose so. After much prayerful consideration, I went ahead and arrived at the course the next day.

Vipassana is a technique of the Theravadan Buddhist meditation lineage, and there are free study centers around the world organized by S.N.
Goenka, an Indian lay-teacher (not a monk) who was raised in Burma.
Goenkaji (as his students refer to him) studied this form of meditation
under a Burmese master named U Ba Khin, and was so deeply impressed
by the method—that of uncovering the true nature of impermanence
(*anicca*)—that he devoted his life and financial resources to setting up
meditation centers all over the world.

The day after I quit my corporate job back in California, I went
straight into my first ten-day Vipassana course. Afterward, I said, "This
is by far THE hardest thing I have ever done in my life." A few months
later, after I had trained for and ran an entire 26.2 mile marathon, I still
said, "Vipassana was even harder." (Incidentally, Vipassana meditation
helped me tremendously during the actual marathon. After about Mile
20, I used "witnessing" techniques of awareness of respiration and sensation in order to *observe* the mental and physical pain rather than identify
with it. It worked, and helped me cross the finish line.)

Believe me—and I know the mothers out there will mark my words—

I feel I could endure a natural delivery if I were to ever have a child. Maybe that's naive of me, but through witnessing techniques, the type of pain I have been able to observe is tremendous.

Part of this Vipassana meditation technique involves not becoming averse to unpleasant ("pain") sensations or attached to and developing craving for lovely little vibrations and tingling sensations ("pleasure"). From Day Four of the course onward, participants must sit in a single posture for one entire hour without moving a muscle.

This may seem completely easy. Yet, consider that you are on your bum for eleven hours a day, sitting on a hard cushion in a position that Westerners are simply not genetically predisposed to tolerate! And that's just the physical challenge; the mental test—asking oneself, "Can I do it? Why am I doing this? Who cares?!"—is another dimension altogether.

In actuality, the silence part—not speaking for ten days—is a beautiful thing. I have come to fully enjoy silence. In fact, since practicing serious meditation, I have become increasingly sensitive to much of the mindless chatter that floats around my head most of the time.

Speaking of chatter, I was thinking a lot, and trying to reel in my monkey mind, swinging from branch to branch. When I wasn't supposed to be thinking, I was thinking how I couldn't wait to start thinking again.

I stayed up at the Vipassana center an extra two days in order to readjust my socially-interactive brain a bit before heading down to the village of McLeod. The best part of an intense retreat is the first day after—walking through the mountains, with the Himalayas towering above, and the green hillside terracing so typical of Asia. Birds chirping, creeks bubbling… it feels like a Technicolor Disney movie. One's senses are so keen and sharp after such deprivation. It's like a super vivid dream!

When I returned to the bustling town of McLeod, it felt like New York City. I wanted to bolt, to catch the next bus out, right away. I felt completely done over, and ready to make a change. Alas, I may have thought I was ready, yet I quickly realized that my mind and coinciding physicality were absolutely 100% exhausted. You may *think* you're not wiping yourself out in retreat because physical activity is almost nil; but in fact, the mental exertion is tremendous. It has taken me at least four days to finally feel back to myself. And of course, the concept of who that is must catch up to the past two weeks of change and self-examination—or make that self-emollition.

There's a little "travel family" of foreign folks from the Vipassana course who have settled into a group guest house. We are all leaving together tonight on a bus that will whistle over potholes to Rishikesh, which lies about twelve hours south of here in the state of Uttarakhand. As for me, I plan on (yeah right, PLAN—that's a laugh in India) finding a little nest in Rishikesh. I would like to stay for a while—maybe a month or more, practicing yoga and enjoying the peace and serenity of this holy pilgrimage site at the headwaters of the River Ganges, the great Mother Ganga.

I'm THRILLED to be heading back into "India proper." As I've described, McLeod is a touristy "Little Lhasa" Tibetan enclave—and a tremendously westernized one at that. It is so cozy and comfortable: pizza parlors, English breakfasts, shops of kitsch, even a makeshift movie hall for the touristas—and that is not what I have traveled halfway around the world to experience. I know Rishikesh will be much more "India."

I look forward to the chaos, the colors that take your breath away, the smells that make you wonder what planet you're on, and the beauty of having to let go and surrender. I only tasted this experience the first four days of my trip (in wacky Delhi) before I whisked myself up to the mountains of McLeod. Now, my real India journey begins anew!

Hare Krishna

13ᵗʰ of December, Rishikesh

It's strange to think that, halfway around the globe, most of America is gearing up for the holidays. Here in Rishikesh, the self-described "yoga capital of the world," there isn't a swath of red or green in sight, no malls to be found, no rosy-cheeked Santas ringing bells. The only bell-ringers are *pujaris* offering the daily *pujas* to Lord Shiva ("puja" technically means "offering" in Hindi) each morning and evening, the jingles and jangles emanating from temples and echoing across the river Ganga.

Lord Shiva is the most worshipped god in India, and holy Rishikesh is quite the hot spot for his worshippers. Shiva is one of the gods in the main Hindu God triad, which includes Brahma the creator, Vishnu the preserver, and Shiva the destroyer. I have many-a-lifetime to go before scratching the surface of identifying the more-than-330 MILLION gods and goddesses in the Hindu pantheon, but I am learning—slowly. So far, I feel most inspired by Ganesh and Saraswati, as well as the "couple of divine love," Krishna and Radha.

Ganesh, also known as Ganapati, is the pink-colored, pot-bellied, elephant-headed god and son of the goddess Parvati and Lord Shiva. In a fit of rage, Shiva the father accidentally lopped off his own son's human head. Out of sheer guilt, Shiva immediately replaced it with the head of the very first animal he came across, which happened to be an elephant.

Ganesh is known as the Divine Remover of Obstacles, a very handy deity to have around! He is always prayed to first, before proceeding with any other rite or ritual. He is of particular importance to travelers and writers, and is also a great bestower of wisdom.

The luminous goddess Saraswati is the consort of Lord Brahma. Maa Saraswati rides a swan and has four to eight arms, depending on the depiction. She holds a stringed instrument called a *veena* on her lap, and several sacred scriptures known as the *Vedas* in her hands. Saraswati is the goddess of learning, teaching, music, knowledge, and all related areas.

Lord Krishna and his lovely consort Radha are all about the love. Krishna seduced a group of milkmaids (*gopis*), of which Radha was the most enticing, albeit (gasp!) married—but that didn't stop them from joining together in a divine play (*lila*); Radha was drunk with divine love (*bhakti*) and couldn't help herself. They both play flutes and the flamboyant, blue-skinned, peacock plume-wearing Krishna is the most gorgeous of all gods. Hare Krishna—it's the real thing!

Room with River View

14ᵗʰ of December, Rishikesh

Here in this holy pilgrimage destination, I feel lucky and blessed to
have found a little bungalow directly on the bank of the Ganges, considered an actual, living goddess ("Ganga Maa," as she is called—the Great
Mother).

My little nook at the riverside guest house costs a whopping 100 Rupees per night (US$2.00). No hot shower, but 24-hour bucket hot water,
and even a Western standard, sit-down toilet (although it doesn't take
long to get your thigh strength and proper stance down for the squat toilets—necessity is the mother of invention). My walls are painted a sweet
robin-egg blue. And directly across from my cozy bed, I can look out the
window to gaze upon the turquoise blue river goddess Herself.

My favorite times of the day in Rishikesh are early morning, just before
the crack of dawn, and in the late evening, for two reasons, both auditory:
The first is that lovely, power-haunting howl the wind makes as it gusts
through the river valley at dawn and late at night. This is especially delightful since the wind stops practically on the dot at noon each day, and
the weather warms up nicely to clear blue skies and welcome sunshine.

The second reason is that, at these two times of day, the omnipresent,
piercing sound of amplified Hindi music disappears. *Ahhhh…* my brain
gives a sigh of relief. Maybe in another life I will learn the secret as to

why Indians seem to need ALL music turned up to the point of distortion. Another secret to be revealed, in a following life, will be the answer to why they feel the need to play the same song over and over and over again, every day, until the tape is eaten by the machine itself.

Or—*tsk-tsk*—a sneaky American girl puts a monkey-wrench into the machinery and snips a wire or two, putting an end to the relentless, deafening squeal of Bollywood blockbuster soundtracks screeching throughout the village.

Vinod, the 22-year-old manager of my guest house, likens himself to a Bollywood film star, complete with Casanova persona and a young Gregory Peck smile. Vinod does a pretty good job of holding down the fort for his foreign visitors. The first night, as we chatted on the terrace, he revealed to me that his one dream—his ONLY dream in life—is getting to America. Personally, I think he should get himself to Bombay instead and land himself a part in one of those Bollywood movies!

Vinod has kindly offered to teach me Hindi—at least enough to feel comfortable and less ignorant during my half-year stay in India. As of today, I am now able to properly count to ten (that took a full week to learn!). I can also say please, thank you, how are you, I'm fine, HOW MUCH? (I am finally learning to bargain), GO AWAY, sugar, cow, camel, monkey, dog, cat, and "My name is Erin."

First on my list for this week is "Where is the loo, please?"

Vinod is of the Brahmin caste of Indians. Brahmins, traditionally the priests or scholars, are considered the "highest" caste in India. The caste system may be frowned upon in politically correct discussions, but is actually still alive and well. Of all the things that have yanked at my heartstrings in India, it is this underlying system of social class and respect (or lack thereof, rather) that has done me in most. There is a little boy who works here at the guest house, Ajay, from Bihar (the poorest state in India). Ajay is on duty 24 hours a day. From what I can tell, he owns one shirt, one pair of trousers, one hat, one pair of flip flops with about a millimeter of tread left in them, and one jacket. His family lives three days away by train; he is probably working to simply earn a roof over his head and two meals a day. We communicate through sign language and smiles.

I am confused by the "servant" (or is that *slave*?) treatment of Ajay. It hurts to see him ordered around like a piece of nothingness. I wanted to lend him my Walkman to play with, but the manager won't allow him to use it. I want to give him a tiny bit of money, but something tells me not to—that there are things about India, and class structure, and servant "systems" that I simply don't understand. The best I can do is observe, learn, send love his way, and treat him with respect and smiles.

But even "lower" than the Bihari servant boy is the caste of "Untouchables," the Harijans, to which Gandhi applied the name "Children of God." The Harijans are the only ones that are allowed to clean toilets. I have to let the guest house know one day before I want my bathroom cleaned in order for them to find "the sweeper"—the Harijan boy. I, of course, took offense to this and immediately spouted off to Vinod that I certainly clean my very own toilet in America. When the sweeper-boy, with impossibly-thin frame and huge eyes bulging out of a skeletal face, came by to clean my toilet, I wanted to cry, hug him, and tell him that he is worthy, lovable, and most certainly *touchable*.

Is it karma? Madness? What is madder than our own insanities and hidden class systems in the West? Can we compare? I don't think so. India and the U.S. have their respective personal sorrows, their joys, their ways of dealing with the human condition. Is one better than the other? More civilized? Certainly these questions are part of the reason I am here, and I'm not sure there is an answer, let alone a correct one.

As Rilke said, we must live the questions:

"I would like to beg you dear Sir, as well as I can, to have patience with everything unresolved in your heart and to try to love the questions themselves as if they were locked rooms or books written in a very foreign language. Don't search for the answers, which could not be given to you now, because you would not be able to live them. And the point is to live everything. Live the questions now. Perhaps then, someday far in the future, you will gradually, without even noticing it, live your way into the answer." (Rainer Maria Rilke, 1903, *Letters to a Young Poet*)

Body Wisdom

15th of December, Rishikesh

It is said that by taking three full dips in the holy River Ganga, all of your sins are washed away. Can't beat that ritual; I'll definitely be partaking. Cold as that mountain stream water may be this December, it's clean and clear here in Rishikesh, near the Ganges' headwaters—much more enticing than downstream Varanasi, home of the cremation grounds, burning ghats and Shiva-knows-what floating down the river. I read in the paper that they have introduced a charred-flesh-eating fish species into the Ganges near Varanasi, to act as a vacuum cleaner for all the corpse remnants. As ghoulish as all this sounds, it's another example of the fascination of Mother India in that She doesn't try to hide Her life, death, suffering, and joy. It's all out there for one to see, smell, and taste.

Right now, I'm focusing on other sensory immersions. Here in Lakshman Jhula, the village where I'm staying, I've found an Iyengar-style yoga teacher I like by the name of Anil. Every day I attend an hour-and-a-half asana class (asana means posture) in the morning, and sometimes, again in the late afternoon. Since it's off-season, I'm usually the only student attending the afternoon class, which gives me both stage fright and the opportunity to get plenty of individual attention.

Iyengar yoga, founded by the infamous yogi and guru B.K.S. Iyengar, is a hatha yoga derivative known for its strict focus on alignment. The emphasis is not on rapid succession of postures; rather, one holds positions for several seconds or even minutes. My main reason for learning asanas while I'm here is the obvious—to improve my health and vitality. Plus, this intensive practice will give me the opportunity to create a "body memory" so that I can practice a yoga routine on my own, anytime, anywhere.

I have three mini-goals for yoga before I leave Rishikesh. First, though I've experimented with yoga off and on for about ten years, due to a strange lack of coordination or lack of commitment, or both, I've never been able to memorize the Surya Namaskar (Sun Salutation) sequence. (Yoga buffs scoff, "Easy as pie!") My first goal is accomplished: I have finally memorized the Sun Salutation asanas, along with synchronized inhales and exhales, which are very important for me, as I am too lazy to do *pranayama*, the breathing exercises that are central to yoga practice.

My other mini-goals are to be able to push myself into a full backbend (*chakra-asana*), and then put myself into (and stay in!) a full headstand (*shirshasana*). Both of these require more strength and balance than I currently have; plus, I need to get past the psychological blocks of turning myself upside-down. I'm sure it's easier than I think. And, these goals are just incidental. The journey is the destination, especially with yoga.

After two weeks of intensive practice, I can already feel myself "lightening up" physically, as well as mentally and spiritually. Upon leaving Dharamsala a couple weeks ago, I was feeling quite blocked, physically stiff and a little emotionally stuck. I had to remind myself: Yes, Erin, it takes TIME to integrate into a new place. Coming to Rishikesh was like coming to a new country altogether—new "vibes," and new water, food, smells, bacteria (oh yeah!), and new culture all the way around.

Speaking of our little internal traveling companion, I experienced my first little bout of bacterial fun last week. It started with a crazy little fever that lasted about five hours. I think I nipped the worst part in the bud by eating a ton of acidophilus and taking a fabulous homeopathic remedy meant to assist with mental or physical duress. When the fever ended, though, I had one mild day of the infamous "Delhi Belly"—the Indian subcontinent's answer to "Montezuma's Revenge." Suffice it to say, I was much luckier than some travelers I've seen around here—three days of stomach problems can turn anyone into a walking skeleton. *That* would be the time to break out the real meds.

Rock Ashram

16ᵗʰ of December, Rishikesh

I've sussed out my favorite find in Rishikesh: the old, abandoned Marahishi Maresh Yogi compound, otherwise touted as "The Beatles' Ashram." What a place. Tucked away just south of the hustle and bustle of the main tourist settlement of Ram Jhula, the Marahishi ashram reminds me of a location straight out of *Lord of the Rings*. It's Middle Earth. There are dozens and dozens of individual meditation huts—pod-like structures resembling Hobbit houses hidden among the hillside foliage. There are gardens and pathways and meditation shrines set against the backdrop of the jungle. (Yes, it is a jungle. I barely managed to avoid the excessive elephant droppings.)

I could only dream of what it was like to be cavorting around this once-splendid ashram during the late 1960's with the likes of John, Paul, George, and Ringo. It must have been a crazy, wild, beautiful scene, and this definitely would have been where I hung out! Upon my own discovery of it, I felt a sense of sadness that it was all over, abandoned. It's almost as if it were too good to be true.

I was told that most of the *White Album* was composed here. One can see the old "Number Nine" room where the Beatles apparently stayed, and the song "Dear Prudence" was apparently written for Mia Farrow's sister, who was holed up in meditation all day. The Fab Four were doing their best to beckon dear Prudence away from her relentless internal quest. "Won't you come out to play?"

If one listens closely to the sounds of India, it's easy to understand the land's influence on the Beatles' music. I recall the odd background sounds and psychedelic samples, especially on *Sergeant Pepper's*. It's India! It's the strange and beautiful concoction of the call of the chai wallah, the incessant bicycle and motorbike horns, the ashram chants over loudspeakers across the river, the clanging Shiva temple bells, the blaring "Bollywood" background music, and so on. Nowhere else on earth is there such an assortment of sounds that actually has a taste, a smell, and a visceral feel—a veritable rock ashram.

Who could blame the Beatles for being so enchanted?

The Rishikesh Effect

2nd of January, Rishikesh

It's happened. I have dropped off the spiritual deep end of India.

For two weeks now, I've tried to leave for south India and escape the cold, to no avail. After several thwarted attempts (power outages, rainstorms, missed connections) to buy a rail ticket, I finally surrendered to the fact that—for now—Rishikesh is my home, and I'm not supposed to leave. A yogi friend of mine, Max from the UK, calls this common phenomenon found among folks who get pulled into the vortex, "The Rishikesh Effect."

It's been exactly one month since my arrival in Rishikesh. I seem to have crossed a real milestone. I now feel such a connection to this place, to the locals, and to the rare remaining foreign "pilgrims" inclined to muscle through the cold weather, staying beyond the tourist high season.

In this holy village, I am having experiences that are seemingly cliché or perhaps simply par for the India journey. Seems as if I'm having a spiritual tune-up of sorts, in spite of my rational mind. In hindsight, I can see that the first few weeks here were really about resistance. I didn't want to admit to things I was feeling in my body and my heart. I have now determined that my normal mental faculties are useless in India! As the rational mind seems to have turned itself OFF, my real guides are the heart and intuition.

Things are happening in the energy centers in my body, called *chakras* ("wheels"). It is believed that the human body has seven main chakras, starting at the base of the spine and going up and out the top of the head. From the bottom up they are root, sacral, solar plexus, heart, throat, third eye, and crown chakra, in that order. A decade ago, I tuned into and worked with these chakras in my own body; in the past few years, however, I have been out of touch and lost interest, focusing on other important elements on my path.

Now, what I am experiencing in Rishikesh is a full-blown reawakening to these energy centers in my body. The heart chakra is opening and expanding, which is significant in that it is the unifying center between grounded earth energies and the higher realms—an integration vortex of sorts. As I live day to day here, I experience spontaneous "burning" in my heart—and, no, it's NOT the chilies in the Indian food. It feels a bit like a stretching, like a lotus flower opening from its bud. It's a visceral sensation on a physical level, without explanation, manipulation, or expectation.

Many people come to Rishikesh to find their "guru," or attune themselves to a specific ashram or body of teachings. For me, my everyday life is my guru, and that the common laborer I chat with in the chai shop for hours on end is as much my spiritual guide as the swami or enlightened master sitting in the front of the *satsang* hall. At least, so far.

An added benefit of being in a place like Rishikesh is that everyone can be as "freaky" or outcast as they want to be! I could walk down the street with wacky face paint resembling the strange markings of a *sadhu*, chanting and skipping if I wanted to, and I'd fit right in with the renunciates and babas living along the Ganga. I haven't been painting my face much—a mild act of liberated freakiness is allowing myself to drop into a spontaneous meditative state no matter where I am, whenever I want. But I'm rarely seen without my trademark *bindi*—stuck right on the *ajna chakra*, the spot where my third eye peers out! That space seems to be wide open now, indeed.

Miracle On the Mangala Express

27th of January, Konkan Coast

One Rishikesh morning, in meditation, it finally came: an inescapably loud thought! A message! It was time to leave! I scampered over to the ashram where Katy, my new British buddy, was staying. I left her a note inviting her to hop aboard a train south with me. Katy had also been seduced by Rishikesh's charms, and had stayed way past her intended date of departure. By no coincidence, she had received the same insight that morning during yoga; it was time to split and escape from the cold. And we knew exactly where we were headed: straight for a rainbow.

At the beginning of December, a little bird told me that a Rainbow Gathering was to be held in the South of India, along the Konkan Coast in Karnataka. I have always wanted to go to a Rainbow Gathering, one of those "bucket list" things to do in this lifetime. A Rainbow Gathering is a family, an international "tribe of many colors" coming together to live harmoniously with each other and with the land. A Gathering is a totally self-sufficient group of interdependent individuals, maintaining their own cooking, music, facilities, contributions, talents, errors, egos, joys, love, and humanity.

Rainbows typically last for one month, from full moon to full moon, with a substantial set-up period preceding and a clean-up period following. Typically, there is one super-grand international gathering with several thousand participants at least one time during the year at a new location around the globe, and other Rainbows are held regionally at other times, sometimes annually in the same location. This particular gathering that Katy and I were headed to was a reunion of a Rainbow last held three years prior in the same location.

For the last three weeks in Rishikesh, Katy and I had considered whether to go south to the Gathering, and the time was finally right. Katy, a 21-year-old bright sprite from England, is actually an ideal travel partner for me right now—a totally independent free spirit with no hang-ups—a well-seasoned traveler who has been making her way around the world for about a year now. Perfect.

Together, we made our somewhat bittersweet goodbyes to the chai wallahs, the blessed Ganges, the holy cows, swamis, sadhus and other humans we had befriended during our six-week stay in Rishikesh. It had become my home; I had to remind myself that I can always return to my little blue room at the guest house in Lakshman Jhula if I want. Such is the nature of my journey sans itinerary.

After a few days of lengthy farewells, Katy and I set off for a four-day haul to find the pot of gold at the end of the Rainbow.

Thus began a mammoth journey in which we went from down jackets and fleece hats to coconuts, pineapples, and tropical paradise. But first, we had to undergo a wild transport adventure involving a rickshaw, a train, a taxi, a train, a bus, a bus, a bus, and, finally, a four-kilometer walk into India's coastal jungle.

The first major leg of the trip involved an overnight train from Haridwar, the main railway hub near Rishikesh, to Old Delhi train station. Typical India: the train arrived in Old Delhi two hours late. As a result we had, literally, only twenty-five minutes to make it ALL THE WAY ACROSS DELHI—the capital city with population of thirteen million!—to Nizamuddin station in the south of the city, before our vital link connecting train was scheduled for departure.

Now, this was a feat for nothing less than superhuman deities. What needed to happen was logistically impossible. We needed our taxi cab to sprout wings, Inspector Gadget-style, and fly across town. As we threw our packs into the car, we both shouted "GO!!!!!!" to the driver at the top of our lungs.

Of course, the price instantly rose 100 rupees out of nowhere, but we didn't care. "JUST DRIVE!!!!" we commanded, again in tandem.

Usually I am quite the optimist, but as we sat in a monstrously huge, seemingly insurmountable traffic jam of cows, scooters, rickshaws, delivery trucks, and taxis for over ten minutes without moving an inch, I had less faith than the size of a sesame seed that we'd make our train. I did notice a sweetly-lighted Ganesh altar blinking on the dashboard of the cab, and silently prayed, "Okay, O Ganapati, great divine remover of obstacles, we need your help!"

The driver kept gunning the little lawnmower engine, then stopping for traffic, hiccupping his way across Delhi in the constantly-stalling morning traffic. I pulled my shawl over my head—I couldn't look. We were at a standstill, another massive confusion of cross-purpose activity, just one block before our train station!

"Get out and RUN! You only having four minutes to get your train!" bellowed our driver. I shoved three hundred-rupee notes in the man's fist and tumbled out of the car, already buckled and strapped into my pack and ready to fly.

Katy and I ran as fast as we could, weaving through traffic and barreling through the crowds. What a sight we were: two crazy-looking, disheveled white women with overstuffed bags, panicked eyes and wild bed-head hair flying everywhere, heaving our way up the steps to the platform crossing, huffing and puffing like we might keel over.

I shouted at the top of my tired lungs, "WE NEED A PORRRRTER!!! SOMEONE HELPPPPP!!!!" as we had absolutely no idea which track the "Mangala Lakshadweep Express" train would be departing from, and the only signs to be seen were in Hindi hieroglyphics. People were not coming forward to help; instead, they were getting out of our way and moving aside. There wasn't a red-vested porter in sight.

A glance at my watch informed me that we had less than thirty seconds left; realizing that no uniformed officials—or anyone for that matter—wanted to assist the crazed Western women, I decided to "punt." I picked a random track that had a bit of activity brewing and went for it! With Katy bringing up the rear, we flew down the steps to a train that looked lengthy and long-distance, praying it was the one! Sweaty, dirty, and desperate, I shouted as we reached the platform, "IS THIS THE MANGALA BLAHBLAHBLAHBITTYBLAH EXPRESS????!!!!!"

The answer, thank God, given to us by a group of Indians wobbling their heads in the affirmative, was YES. As we stepped on the train, it immediately started moving beneath our feet. Not a second to spare.

Over the Rainbow

28th of January, Konkan Coast

Two days of rickety-rail-riding later, we alighted in the dark, wee hours to discover a completely new India—the South. The thick night air was WARM and humid; we could smell flowers! An ice cream man was the only thing open for business. Talk about a contrast to the wintery North. Katy and I luxuriated with showers and a good night's sleep at the railway station's retiring room, setting out at sun-up to find our way to the Rainbow Gathering.

It really is amazing that we found this place, sparse instructions written swiftly by another traveler, scratched out on the back of a worn-out piece of paper. We could only pray that the bus drivers knew what-the-heck village we're talking about, as we lugged our over-packed rucksacks through aisles of curious, wide-eyed Indians, the only Westerners in sight, aware that too much skin is showing but unfortunately lacking a free hand to cover up, sweating puddles, as the bus whistles through the jungle toward God-knows-where. We knew we had to just "turn it over." Wherever we ended up, we would deal with it!

We were dumped off at the end of the bus line near a lagoon, then followed our noses and the negligible notes for four back-breaking kilometers (will I ever learn the art of packing light?) through a jungle to one super secluded, infinitely magical stretch of coastline. There, we finally found our new community of groovy folks living on a beach straight out of a movie set, complete with turquoise blue ocean, arching palms, and about a hundred or so very colorful, very happy people.

The kitchen and a few small living areas had been hollowed out of tightly clustered coconut tree groves, with hammocks strung between trees and straw mats strewn hither and thither.

I walked around, checking it all out, unsure where to begin or what to do. I heard a friendly voice say, "Welcome home, sister. Put your pack down and come down to the water for sunset!"

It was a sparkly blue-eyed, cute-as-a-bug Kiwi, barefoot and barely twenty. With his homemade clothes and feathers tied in his hair, he looked like just a wood spirit, exuding nothing but pure love. I immediately felt at home, thanks to him. I chained my backpack to a coconut tree and dove right into the Gathering.

Katy and I stayed at the Rainbow through the closing full moon and beyond, into the clean-up period until final completion. During our time at the Gathering, I encountered new ways of conflict resolution and group decision-making: vision circles using a Native American talking stick. I had used talking sticks before, but not involving a hundred personalities! I learned how to make *chapati* (Indian flat bread), and *seera* (semolina porridge) in an assembly line, enough for a peaceful army. I soaked in the sun, swam in the sea, slept under the stars, and filled my soul with lovely live music, drumming, dancing, firedancers and firelight. I witnessed ways to be a part of a huge family, scratching the surface as to how to live in a close-knit community without losing one's independence—or one's sanity.

Interestingly, there were only three Americans out of about two hundred Westerners that came and went during the course of the Gathering. In general, Americans are scarce along the travel routes of India. On this trip, I've met more people from Belgium, and even Brazil, than the U.S. Of course, there are some political reasons for this, including the fear that has been instilled by governments about international affairs. Also, with the exception of the most popular vacation destinations, Americans simply don't travel abroad near as much as Europeans, Australians, or even Canadians. This contributes to the fact that the average American is notably less worldly-minded and internationally-aware than other nationalities, for better or worse.

Enough of socio-politics; I digress!

Back to the Rainbow!

As the closing full moon of the Gathering drew near, Katy and I talked it over and absolutely agreed that it was a good idea to stay through the clean-up period—to continue to learn and observe, and to work and contribute even more, to give back to those who carried the vision and were such powerful examples of "servant leadership." It was touching to see the group shrink in size, slowly, slowly over the final three days, to a hard-core clean-up crew of twenty. The final morning, our small tribe held hands in a circle over the remnants of the main fire, offering a closing prayer of thanks and a final "Om." We then loaded ourselves into a (prearranged) local boat to be carried across the sea to the nearest beach with amenities; in other words, someone else to cook, and a proper place to shower.

Twenty of us climbed aboard the flimsy fisherman's craft. Like the miracle on the Mangala Express, here was another instance of waning faith. A rickety boat straight out of Robinson Crusoe, with a tiny putt-putt motor attached. Would it hold?

We were a sight to see, piling onto this poetic little wooden ship—dreadlocks, grimy clothes, djembe drums, beat-up travel guitars and what-have-yous, and the full-on colorful sight of twenty freaks *au naturel*, some who hadn't left the beach in over thirty days. Man, oh, man, that boat was rocking. There was a huge chance we'd capsize. The Indian man kept yelling at us to stay down in the base of the boat, his little boy running from stern to prow, back and forth, end to end to balance out the weight! We were tipping! And still, the temptation to peek out from the hull was too great, as dolphins swam by, leaping through the air, welcoming us safely to our new home on the next shore.

Chai Break

29ᵗʰ of January, Konkan Coast

I've been "on the road" Jack Kerouac-style for the past two weeks.

And now, I've landed somewhere over the rainbow, on a very quiet south Indian beach on the Konkan Coast. I'm typing this from an open-air computer "hut" with the sound of the Indian Ocean's waves crashing in the background. The weather is about 30-degrees Celsius, a comfortable mid- to high-80s for the Fahrenheit folks. Coconut trees abound; the water is bathtub warm, and the breeze continually refreshes. My most recent days have been spent lazing and lolling, alternating between my mud hut (less than one dollar a night), my hammock underneath the coco trees, and my straw mat laying a few steps away at the foot of the lapping waves. Life is good!

I am currently on a cleansing fast of sorts—consuming nothing more than a few bananas and lemon water. This fast idea arose spontaneously over the last four days as I developed another small bout of "Delhi Belly"—diarrhea, fever, aches, cramps, the works. It was only horrific for two days, which seems to be a much swifter recovery than some folks' accounts. I attribute this to the Chinese herbs I bought in San Francisco's Chinatown, and homeopathic remedies to bring down fever.

Since the cleansing process of the body began organically, I've decided to continue and give my body a needed breather from the rigors of travel fare, most especially chai. I've consumed a small tea plantation since landing in Delhi. I'm on serious overload, having developed an addiction to the sickly sweet, devilishly delicious concoction of *masala* spices, black tea, milk and sugar, milk, sugar, milk, milk, sugar, sugar. Oh, and did I add: milk and sugar?

Yep, time for a chai break.

Guru Disney

22ⁿᵈ of February, Konkan Coast

I've just returned to paradise after a whirlwind side trip—back in my discovered little beach oasis on the Arabian Sea along the southwest coast of India. I can't get enough of sleeping in my "plush" hammock-nest, camping out of my luxurious mud hut quarters, waking up to magnificent sunrises under the coconut trees, bowing before mind-blowing sunsets, devouring entire juicy papayas in one go, skipping barefoot, and dancing in the waves.

It's simply fantastic to be back in this magical locale after a one-week excursion that may have taught me, yet again, one of the most valuable lessons for me in India: the return to self. Before I begin the tale, allow me to lay out a few "disclaimers." First, I haven't fully digested the experience and, I wouldn't be surprised AT ALL if my perspective does a complete flip-flop in the near or distant future. Second, this is MY experience. I do not judge nor wish to analyze another's path or viewpoint. The beauty of travel—of life, of the path to self-discovery—is that things are constantly evolving within and without.

Ever heard of "Osho"? Perhaps the name Bhagwan Shree Rajneesh rings a bell. Rajneesh was labeled as the "sex guru" at one time—the charismatic, funky skullcap- and sunglass-sporting spiritual leader with long white beard. In the early 1980's, Rajneesh owned dozens of Rolls-

Royces and enticed thousands of seekers (*sannyasins*) to leave all behind and join his famed commune, "Rajneeshpuram" up in Oregon.

In 1985, Rajneesh was exiled from the U.S. on grounds of misconduct and violation of immigration laws, although some devotees claim CIA tampering and gradual poisoning. Rajneesh returned to his homeland of India, dropped the old identity of Bhagwan and, *voila*, became simply "Osho"—new look, new name, new image. Osho's ashram empire was rebuilt in Pune, a city of three million lying about three hours west of Mumbai (Bombay) in the state of Maharashtra. Osho left his body in 1990, but the ashram, known as "Club Med-itation," lives on, bigger and juicier than ever before.

When I was in Rishikesh at Christmastime, a fellow traveler gifted me with a daily meditation book by Osho, *Alone We Fly*. The simple, inspiring words and insights made sense and drew me in. Plus, the philosophy was exciting! Follow your bliss! Find out! It resonated; after all, the Buddha encouraged people to investigate the truth rather than rely on hearsay. Not only that, I'm quite the curious cat. After traveling in India for a while, hearing much of the Osho controversy and the words of skeptics, distant admirers, and a few loyalists, I figured there was only one way to find out what was really going on behind those ashram gates: go there. It would be a sort of "spiritual investigative journalism." Was it brainwashing? Absolute rubbish? Were people really having tantric sex on the lawn? I decided to dive in and discover the truth.

After the Rainbow Gathering, I indulged in one month of pure beach peace and perfection. Lest I find myself "stuck" in tropical paradise for the remainder of my India journey, I decided I better pry myself off my duff and get moving. It's backpacker nature to get stuck. There are two sides to the "stuck" phenomenon: sometimes you've simply got to motivate yourself or you'll never see more of the country you've traveled halfway around the world to experience; on the other hand, if you're blissfully happy, why change it? It's really a western mindset that we must "be productive" and "do," rather than just BE. I think I've learned, through recent events, that it's better to ride the wave of bliss while it's up rather than unnecessarily extricate oneself from ecstasy.

In any case, I'm neither so evolved nor distant from western thinking yet. Although I almost skipped the rail reservation altogether, I reluctantly packed up the mud hut and loaded my rucksack at dawn to board an overnight sleeper train headed north to Pune, in the state of Maharashtra. It is here in this polluted metropolis that the great and famous Osho Ashram is found.

Half asleep, I deboarded the train at sunrise, and the rickshaw dumped me off at the ashram gates. I wandered around the outskirts of the compound in the dark, riling up a cacophony of dogs and waking up servants and housewives until someone offered me a decent room. At midmorning, I entered the ashram, feeling things out, and discovered I'd landed smack dab in the middle of a spiritual theme park of sorts. It was "Guru Disney"—with steep Western prices to prove it.

Though I reminded myself to keep an open mind and not to judge too quickly, I recoiled from the pretentious, commercial energy of the place—a far cry from the natural environs of the beach paradise I'd just left. By simply observing goings-on while sitting in the cafe outside the Osho Commune International, I got the sense that this enormous ashram was Big Business at its finest and most clever. Unexpectedly, I was hit with a massive dose of culture shock: I felt as if I had been prematurely ripped away from the India I have come to adore. Everything at the ashram was so orderly, so costly, and so *clean* to boot. Where were my cows? My cheap *thali* plates of rice and *dal* lentils? I felt as if someone had catapulted me back to the West without warning—Western prices, clothing, rules and regulations, and a palpable, lingering thirst for a different sort of distraction hung in the air, Euro-American style—here at Club Med-itation.

Still, I'd come all this way and as I don't back down easily, I figured I'd go full gangbusters and see what it was all about. I paid an exorbitant amount (the equivalent of what I could live off in "local" India for one week) just for entry into the resort-cum-ashram on the initial "Welcome Day." This "welcoming" included mandatory passport photos for I.D., mandatory HIV test (to be renewed every three months), an orientation "sampler plate" of meditations, and a tour for "Osho newbies." That would be me.

But before the orientation began, I had to buy the famous robes: two maroon robes for day wear, one white for the special "meeting" in the evening. Luckily, my budget traveler's nose sniffed out an opportunistic little Indian man who had set up a cottage industry selling second-hand robes, squatting in a corner of my apartment complex. I scored three robes for a total of one hundred rupees instead of shelling out five hundred rupees *each* at the snazzy "Galleria" shop located inside the ashram grounds.

The next day, however, I didn't get off so cheap. I had to purchase a mandatory maroon bikini in order to use the swimming pool and the official ashram shop was probably the only place in the entire nation that would sell such a thing.

Now properly outfitted with robes and bikini, I'd do my best to fully immerse myself into the experience. While keeping one eye on my sanity and inner compass, I endeavored to keep a beginner's mind—an open mind—and an open heart. The thousands of devotees (the most by far were Germans mixed with smatterings of other northern Europeans) were *so* sincere. Serious *sannyasins* have dropped their given names in place of an Osho-blessed name of Sanskrit origin, such as "Shakti," "Ananda," or "Prema." My question was, now that Osho is gone, who chooses the names? Half-jokingly, I thought to myself, they're probably randomly generated by computer.

I felt alone and estranged, pressured from the inside and out when I tried to get to know some of the devotees or expressed my concerns, doubts or criticisms. Often they just seemed to look at me, or through me, as if I just hadn't "got it" yet, whatever "it" was. A few *sannyasins* explained from their vast wisdom that I needed to stick around for a few weeks—or *months*—so that my energies could synchronize with the energy of Osho and the ashram. *Okay...I'll do my best.*

Wearing maroon robe at all times, I participated in several different "active meditation" sessions over the course of the week—all techniques approved by Osho before he died, including Sufi (dervish-whirling), Kundalini, Nataraja (Shiva's dance), a variation of Vipassana, and Dynamic Meditation to start the day.

In case you thought meditation was about staying still and keeping quiet, you haven't come across anything like "Dynamic Meditation." Starting at six a.m. was one wild combo of: (1) intense nose-clearing *pranayama*-type breathing with mandatory handkerchief handy—great for eliminating Pune pollution; (2) jumping up and down with arms held high overhead, shouting "HOO HOO HOO HOO!" over and over and over again, enabling the energy to slam down into your lower chakras, awakening life force; (3) gibberish talking, screaming, yelling and letting go of whatever "madness in the mind" you can express; (4) freezing your body in whatever position you find yourself when the gong sounds and holding that pose; and, last but not least, (5) dancing freely in celebration and culmination. Now THAT'S what I call one hell of a creative way to start the day!

I went over the edge during the evening meditation, known as "The Gathering of the White Robe Brotherhood." The name itself gave me the creeps.

Shortly after sunset, one is to arrive inside the main meditation hall, the "Osho Auditorium," freshly showered and wearing a clean, white robe. Then, the ashram gates officially shut—no one allowed in or out. All attendees remain inside this huge pyramid with black marble floors resembling a massive mausoleum. For the next two hours, I struggled to understand what was happening—and when it was all over, I found myself sitting on the floor of the pyramid amongst thousands of white-robed devotees, and said out loud to myself, "That was the most bizarre fucking thing I have *ever* experienced!"

Why wasn't I "getting it"? Why didn't I "get" the need to talk gibberish and scream out angst, then "fall down like a sack of potatoes" the next minute, in order to silence my mind? Why didn't I get the jokes Osho told his "Beloveds" from the huge movie screen projected overhead, as the white-robed folks surrounding me giggled with glee at the words of their Master? Why did I, in contrast to the direction people were purportedly heading, feel increasingly crazier with each passing day, instead of experiencing a deeper inner silence from releasing my madness as promised?

I met an angel along the way—they always show up in our lives when we need them most. John was an older bloke from London of about 60, a very nice and, more importantly, a very witty middle-aged gent with shoulder-length white hair and rosy Santa Claus cheeks. British John had been doing this Osho "trip" for over 25 years, including the years in Rajneeshpuram in Oregon. He was one of the only abnormally-normal sannyasins that seemed keen on speaking with a fringe visitor—an outsider like myself. One day, as we munched lunch together in the cafeteria, John admitted that he'd come to realize that the trip was over for him. He was done with the scene; any of the original magic was gone and it was now about Big Business and New Age Kindergarten—to use his own words. It was one of the most sincere talks I'd had yet at the ashram, and I was overjoyed to have met him.

A few days later, he passed me on the street as I was buying a coconut to suck down. "Hey John!" I shouted, calling him over. "I think I gotta buy a bus ticket outta here—*tonight.*" I saw myself reflected in his eyes, looking increasingly drained and pinched. John lightly took my arm and gently took me to the side of the footpath where we could speak away from the passing ruckus. "Get out, Love," he told me. "You don't need this place. You have a beautiful energy, and it will suck you dry."

He'd validated my senses, my intuition, and my truth. With that boost of encouragement—coming from an old-timer, at that!—I breathed a big sigh of relief. I had my answer. My truth was solid. I rounded the corner to the next travel agent and bought myself a ticket for an overnight bus departing just four hours later—back to the beach.

Now that I'm settled back in paradise, I've talked to a few folks about my experience at the Osho Ashram. Some of the more "grounded" folks well-acquainted with Osho's teachings assure me that the current ashram is a far, far cry from what the Teacher himself taught or envisioned. They agree that, indeed, big business has taken over since his death and the sincere message and enlightening energy have been whittled away. My gut tells me this is true. And, my gut tells me something else, as Osho himself pointed out:

G-U-R-U stands for "Gee, you are you."

More and more, I have got the message to take the spiritual trip less seriously—I've already "got it." So here I am, back on the beach, to enjoy myself, to celebrate "getting it." I also feel the need to regenerate and refuel body, mind, and spirit after getting a bit beat up out there in Guru Disney.

Yet, contrast certainly has its place: This morning, waking up in my hammock to the rooster crowing, hearing the waves crash against the shore, eying a cow munching her morning compost scraps, staring up at the palm trees—all was right with the world. I had returned to my ashram, and Mother Nature was granting me the sweetest discourse—no robe required. And I have a date with a mango that's calling my name.

What are my plans now? Ha! I heard somewhere that plans are God's sense of humor—and I've found that to be doubly true in India.

By the way, there was no sex on the lawn. At least that I saw.

Heading North

10ᵗʰ of March, Goa

Oh, how I relished the beach paradise "ashram." I cleared the Osho trip from my head, happily munching bananas and frolicking along the shore. Perhaps of all places I've been in India, I have felt the most peaceful on the beach. No big surprise. Mental note to self: I am a beach bum, a California Girl. And, in spite of a desire to laze away the days, I've got this thing inside that feels so "western" and so "old-me" programming. Whenever I'm ultra-cozy and truly comfy, it's, "Uh-oh! Time to uproot myself lest I get stuck here in this hut, this hammock, this haven! India isn't about complacency! I'm here to learn, not to veg out!"

Okay—the beach was starting to get a little boring, too.

So, on the spur of the moment—my travel M.O.—I decided to catch a train up north to Uttar Pradesh, winging it on getting tickets to Varanasi, the most holy city in Hindu India, without reservation. Shivaratri, the high festival celebrating the God of Creation and Destruction himself, was coming up soon, and I'd met a pair of Israeli guys, fresh out of the army, who were going to hop on whatever train they could squeeze into—a potentially hellish three-day, third-class journey—in order to make it to Varanasi in time for the celebrations. These two wanted to be thick in the middle of the power and chaos of the ancient city ruled by Lord Shiva.

As chance has it, I was meant to take a detour. On the train headed north, I ran into Monica, a fun-loving Italian I knew from the beach, who was getting off in the renowned party state of Goa. "Stop in Goa!" she convinced me. "Come dance!"

I hadn't yet visited this Christian "island" of a state—a place where meat and alcohol were fine with the religion, the white sandy beaches beckoned, and hedonists found their stomping grounds. Admittedly Goa, a former Portuguese colony just south of Bombay, had intrigued me. I had sidestepped the state because of a reputation for being too touristy, too busy, and too expensive, with too many Yahoos. But now, apparently, I was ready to yahoo a bit, too. It didn't take much for Italian Monica to twist my arm. Hop off the train I did—and proceeded to spend ten sunny, holiday days in North Goa between the beaches of Anjuna and Arambol. Goa is famous for its trance scene, and I was able to "get my groove on," barefoot on the sand, a few nights in paradise. As much as I like to turn my nose up at tourist trap entertainment, I needed it.

After about a week of mild hedonism and pure indulgent comfort, the original bug to get-thee-to-Varanasi was still biting me in the ass. I still had time to "get intimate" with one more locale in India before leaving for Thailand, and I thought I'd take three luxuriant weeks to settle in to Varanasi—also known as Benaras or Kashi—and really feel the place. Since I'd missed Shivaratri and the Israeli guys were long gone, I booked a horrific, solo three-day train ticket to get me up north in time for the next major festival, the full moon of Holi.

I had been warned about Varanasi; travelers would tell tales about "Shiva's city," and how "everyone gets sick," "stuff will come up," and "it's super intense." But I wasn't afraid. No, not me. "Oh, I'm ready for it. I'm 'Tough Girl' now—been almost five months on the road. Give it to me, India. Show me your stuff, Shiva."

As the saying goes, be careful what you ask for.

Holiday in Holi Hell

22nd of March, Varanasi

Upon first arriving, I was enchanted by Varanasi, one of the world's oldest living cities, with the river goddess, Ganga Maa, meandering at her steps. It was great to be off the beaches for a change, and I was immediately smitten with the richness of romantic, "typical India" in all Her glory. Thrilled to be tap-dancing gaily through the narrow paths of the Old City, I ambled over fresh, steaming cow patties and competed for right-of-way with the largest milking cows I'd ever seen. I delighted in downing tiny cups of syrupy sweet chai at every corner for 1.5 rupees (about three cents) a glass, thrust in the midst of ear-splitting Hindi music blaring over every shopkeeper's loudspeaker:

> Om Namah Shiva!
> Om Namah Shiva!
> Hari Hari Hari!
> Om Namah Shiva!

I asked the boatman who took me for a 5:30 a.m. sunrise float on the Ganga why Indians feel they MUST play the music at such constantly high, distorted levels. He explained, "It's so everyone can ENJOY, no matter where they are in the city." A reasonable answer. Couldn't argue with that one.

After months of being on the road, I praised myself as a strong, street-smart, savvy backpacker chick. "Look, ma! See how easily I circumnavigate this pile of cow shit? See how effortlessly I let the incessant taunting of touts, hecklers, and rip-off artists roll off my back? See how I find this quaint little room with river view for eighty rupees (US$1.50) a night in this sweet little guest house hidden away from the main drag?"

I was digging it. I was an off-the-beaten-track, solo traveling force to be reckoned with, and no one was about to tell me that Shiva's city could kick my ass.

Clearly, I was getting cocky. It was time to be right-sized. And Lord Shiva did the job.

It's all true, what they say. Varanasi is the most intense place I've been in India. It IS the city of Shiva—the most revered, feared, and worshipped god in the Hindu pantheon. He is both the destroyer and the nurturer, and he hits hard both ways. Shiva is about power, and respecting that power, and he taught me a powerful lesson indeed.

A few days after arrival, I sat on the banks of the river, adoring the view of the polluted city and the Ganga with her dead cow corpses and human cadavers floating downstream, watching the Brahmins perform their prayer rituals, their *artis*, at sunset, while the heat—inside and out of my body—became beyond unbearable. I turned to a traveling woman I had befriended, 24-year-old Niki from England, and said in all sincerity, "I feel like I've been drugged." We were powerless to move, watching the holy men circle their cobra-head candelabras up and around their heads, inhaling billowing clouds of incense as they wafted up to where we were, just above the crowds. My mind was swirling. My heart was beating fast in my chest. I had been bitten by the cobra and the city got hotter and harder with each passing hour.

The next night I went down to the burning ghats, where they burn bodies twenty-four hours a day, making sure the skull explodes before the ashes are offered to the Ganga. Death is everywhere. The burning ghat was a peaceful place. I didn't feel pained by being there. It just helped me to realize that death is the flip side of life. It's Nature, and we are not separate.

Upon arriving at the holy city, the message I received through meditation was that "daily life is enough." I did not need to challenge myself to do yoga, or anything that required more effort than buying fruits and veggies, staying reasonably healthy, eating and sleeping and bathing. It wasn't just a physical test. I went through the emotional wringer as well—I could barely keep it together. Mentally? It doesn't apply. The mental mind is blown to bits in Varanasi. There is no space; no time for logical or rational thought. Varanasi simply needs to be "lived through."

After five days, I began deteriorating. I couldn't breathe. I couldn't find my "space." A strange, crooked little Indian man would show up outside my guest house door several times a day: "Hello friend," he'd croak through red, betelnut-stained teeth, with a crazed look in his beady little eyes. "Massage today?" "NO! *Nahi!* NO!" I'd fire back. Then I'd be flashed by "devout" Hindu bathing men on the Ganga, men who didn't know what to do with their sexuality—repressed beyond control as they wait years for their arranged marriages. I felt sick and turned away, hardly in the mood to cater to their delusions that a white girl was going to appreciate the sight of their family jewels.

Finally, Holi kicked off with a bang for three days of sheer upheaval: The most boisterous festival in all of Northern India is feted with bonfires at midnight, followed by days of drinking whiskey and shooting colored paint water on each other. All guidebooks advise tourists—especially women, who tend to get groped—to stay indoors.

As the festival energy was building and boiling, young revelers would threaten to color bomb us as we tried to make our way through the streets. Shrieks of laughter emanating from groups of boys, yelling in Hindi ("You play Holi?") were startling, as they taunted us with water balloons and water pistols filled with colored paint at every turn. The children's antics were tolerable and even bordered on sweet as their faces lit up with innocence, play and laughter. The spray-painted kids in all their colors and glory reminded me of Halloween-time festivities in America. It's the whiskey-swilling, *bhang*-ed up men I was concerned about, *bhang* being a super potent form of *ganja* that is consumed heavily during Holi.

Finally, I had to admit: the whole stewpot was too much for me. On the morning of the day the moon was full—the peak of the festival—I awoke covered in sweat. The sun was blazing, and I was sweltering well before 7 a.m. I got up, overdressed in enough clothes to cover my arms and legs thoroughly—because this is north India we're talking about here, not the beach, and a woman cannot show her skin without more hassle and stares. With a dazed look on my face, I headed next door to Niki's room, knocked, and she opened it. Niki's own glazed-over eyes looked out at me from a face that had seen cheerier days—and I knew she was in the same state as I. If we had turkey oven thermometers stuck in our brains, they would have been popping out with a bang: "DONE!"

We headed over to the travel agency, dodging paint splatterers and stepping in puddles of piss and god-only-knows-what substance, and proceeded to book a train outta there for the very next day—festival or no festival. We were out.

I had planned on staying three weeks. I had lasted seven days. I was not immune to the transformative power of Varanasi. The full moon was exactly 4:05 p.m. (India time)—the exact hour I was blessed with the onslaught of my very own special case of Varanasi "Delhi belly," now renamed by me as "Shiva's revenge." "Well, that's gonna make for an interesting overnight train journey," I said to myself.

My theory about getting ill and enduring diarrhea in India is that heavy-duty traveling holds "too much information" to process, and the body has got to let go somehow; it's an emotional-spiritual detoxification turning physical. I believe that when we accept this process, it becomes a whole lot easier to endure, to nurse ourselves, and let it pass—no pun intended. Of course it's important to be cautious and sensible, but it's much, much deeper than lack of sanitation standards or cooking conditions. Rather than worrying about food poisoning at every turn (which definitely restricts one from enjoying India's culinary discoveries), it's easier to remember that it's about digesting the intensity of experiences and sensory input while on the road.

Keeping all this in mind, with train ticket in hand, I bucked-up, accepting my tricky tummy. Niki and I hopped on the night train in the middle of the Holi festival. Actually, traveling smack-dab on a peak festival night made for a fairly quiet, unpacked train ride to Delhi, which was nice for a change—and good for me as I had to climb out of my upper berth several times during the night to tend to toilet needs. My little Varanasi souvenir, keeping me humble, and letting me know who's really the boss.

"Three Trips to India"

29th of March, Dharamsala

I was amazed at how simple and easy, how *mild* Delhi was after experiencing Varanasi in full-festival mode! I marveled at how far I had
come since that glorious, freaky, terrifying, invigorating night I landed
in Delhi five months ago—this time around, Delhi was a piece of cake!

After convalescing and recovering in Delhi an extra day, I opted to
return even further north to the green, to Nature, to Dharamsala, and
take it easy for my last week. From the heat of the beach, via the crucible
fire of Varanasi, to the Himalaya cold; from the south India seas, via
the burning ghats, to the mountains. From Shiva's stomping grounds to
the peaceful exile of HH the XIV Dalai Lama—no wonder my psyche is
spinning. My body, mind, and spirit are on one hell of a wild ride and
they aren't sure which country, which religion, which food, which tem-
perature, which internal equilibrium we're shooting for here! But that's
what makes traveling in India what it is: special—and full of it all.

Back in November during my very first week in India, an old-time
French-Canadian traveler named Paul, who has been coming to India
since the mid-70's, educated me with a very telling statement, and I've
kept it in the back of my mind ever since. He said, "Erin, there are three
trips you take to India: the one you think you're going to have—that you
plan for; the one you actually have; and the one you live through once

you go back home." Right on, brother. I hear you, and I'm mid-course. I look forward to digesting the super-sized-spoonfuls I'm currently swallowing once I'm back at home.

One pre-meltdown day in Varanasi, I remember thinking to myself, "Oh, how I love India, and She loves me right back!" This *is* very true—I feel nothing but embraced and cared for in this land, very "taken care of" as I surrender to Her totality. I know Mother India still loves me back, even after She's had Shiva whip me back into shape. Goodbye, grandiosity. Hello again, humility!

The Legacy of Impermanence

2ⁿᵈ of April, Rishikesh

I think of Browning's sonnet, "How do I love thee? Let me count the ways. I love thee to the depth and breadth and height the soul can reach..." This is how I feel about India. I am absolutely smitten with this land, Her people, Her senses, Her senses *beyond* the senses.

Last week in Dharamsala, I had the good fortune of seeing the Dalai Lama as he administered his annual public teachings. Ironically, I couldn't sit still for long, even in His Holiness' peaceful presence. My soul told me there was one more stop to make during my last week in India, so off I went for one last heart-stopping, no-sleep-'til-dawn overnight bus ride back to Rishikesh, which felt like a second home. After grueling Varanasi, it was pure healing to come back to Rishikesh, near the headwaters of the river Ganga, where the living goddess flows fresh and clean, straight from the Himalayan source.

Returning to the "Yoga Capital of the World" was beautiful. I saw Rishikesh through new eyes. I felt so much more "Indian"—more accustomed to the people, the ways, the gestures and subtleties that let you know you are really "a part of" a place. My heart burst with joy at the sight of the clean Ganges. The village of Lakshman Jhula was bustling with tourists this time around, unlike the abandoned "local" feel during the winter, but that was fine by me.

Rishikesh was a perfect place for me to spend my final days in India—a way of truly coming full circle. And, there was another reason I returned to this place. His name was Anil, meaning "air" or "wind" in Sanskrit. Anil is about the closest thing to a guru I've experienced on my journey.

During winter, I'd spent about six weeks learning yoga in Rishikesh. I'd met Anil, a 24-year old Iyengar-style yoga instructor, after I had tried three other Indian teachers. Anil was the one for me. His energy was clear, there were no "ego trips" involved, and he had the right balance of challenge and gentleness. Anil moved like a willow tree. He was as flexible as a contortionist, while exhibiting strength and passion for the technique.

I loved being in Anil's presence, especially before we started class. In addition to practicing *hatha*, Anil appeared to be on the *bhakti* path of devotion. He had surrendered his life and his love to Krishna. Early mornings, as the three or four of us regular students straggled in and settled into the icy cold, small and simple practice room, Anil would already be seated in silent meditation before his altar. Anil had a deep connection to God in the form of Lord Krishna, and he was channeling that love and faith to us by teaching us yoga asana. Anil accepted incidental payment for the courses as an aside; once, he told me that money wasn't necessary if one couldn't pay. His main purpose was to pass something on of substance—if a student took back just a little something back to the West after studying with him, he had accomplished what he set out to do, and that was to share the gift of yoga.

After I had been studying with Anil for about a month, he fell ill seemingly out of nowhere, and quickly exhibited a rapid turn for the worse. Starting out with a cold and fatigue, then a swollen throat and painful neck, his beautiful body and light began to deteriorate before our eyes. He never complained, and he would shake off any inquiries. One morning I showed up for class and Anil, looking pale and gaunt, said to me, "Erin, today you be my body to show the new people. I can't do head stand or shoulder stand." The next day, and the day after that, his yoga studio was locked. The landlord told us students that Anil was too ill to teach further. Every day I returned to the studio, but Anil never returned. I wished him the best, then headed south for the Rainbow Gathering and better weather for my own health.

Two months after I had left Rishikesh I was sunning myself in the south when I received a terribly unexpected email from my friend Chris, a Canadian fellow yoga student who was still in Rishikesh: he had just been informed that Anil had passed away suddenly in the night. He had no further information. I was stunned.

Looking back, it seems to me that Anil's beautiful glow, his etheric presence was a spiritual preparation—consciously or unconsciously, it doesn't matter—for entering *mahasamadhi*. Mahasamadhi, according to Hinduism, is a God-illumined master's conscious exit from the body at the time of physical death. It is as if Anil "knew" on some level that he was soon to leave his body.

During the very first class I took with Anil, I had an experience that indicated the depth of his spiritual development. Since I was about seventeen years old, at very random occasions, I have been able to see currents of white light—an aura-like field—surrounding my body, with no particular rhyme or reason as to when it appears. The light stream only lasts for a short instant; I can't control it nor define it, yet, whenever I see it, I feel it's a validation of sorts that I'm definitely in the right place, at the right time, heading in the right direction for my soul's evolution. Even if I'm feeling low, or scared, or uncertain, when I see this "etheric halo," I get the message that all is well and it's all unfolding perfectly. About halfway into my first yoga class with Anil, while I was holding *trikonasana* (triangle pose), I saw this light emanating off my body and got the message: my soul was happy in this class. I was in the right place at the right time with the right teacher.

During my yoga studies, Anil explained to me that when he first started practicing Iyengar-style yoga at the age of eighteen, he was not a strong man and far from super healthy. He could barely touch his toes!

After about four years of intensive training with his guru, Anil opened his doors to western students. He told me that when he first had the impetus to teach foreigners in Rishikesh, he could not speak English. He could understand the language, but when it came to speaking, something was blocked. As he tells it, God unblocked his throat chakra so that he was ultimately able to speak adequately and clearly enough to pass on the valuable teachings of yoga.

Something about the simplicity and definitive compassion in Anil's teaching voice imprinted his instructions into my brain and into my cellular memory. Long after I'd left Rishikesh and headed down to the south of India, I could hear his voice telling me to "Inhale, exhale!" and "Keep *prana* inside!" and "*Rise* up the chest!" and always, "Keep back STRAIGHT!" as I muddled my way, solo, through the routine on the beach. Even before I'd heard that Anil had been deathly ill, I had been sending him *metta*, loving-kindness and vibrations of light and gratitude in my daily meditations.

According to the email I received about Anil's death, no one was particularly clear on the actual "cause." At the young age of 24, my light-bodied yoga teacher was gone. What a strange sensation—a definite reminder of impermanence, to have your personal "example of health" leave the planet so suddenly!

Needless to say, returning to Rishikesh toward the end of my India journey has given me a chance to say goodbye to Anil in my own way. I attended another teacher's yoga classes—getting a little inspiration again. And I made sure to pass by Anil's former studio to pay my respects. "Thank you, my teacher," I whispered, as I hung a garland of marigolds on the door in gratitude for the lessons of a lifetime that he shared with me so selflessly. A bittersweet farewell, a direct experience of impermanence mixed with everlasting legacies.

Off to Delhi to catch a red-eye to Thailand. But this is far from the end. Thank God I have a ten-year visa—courtesy of the U.S. consulate and the envy of every non-American Indophile in the Western world.

Future Shock

6th of April, Bangkok

Landing in Bangkok, I was shocked. Friends who have traveled this route before told me that after India, Thailand would seem like the West, or "the future." Still, I wasn't prepared for the extreme contrast to my grungy, raw, beloved India. I've had to give myself a tough talking-to in order to not compare. After all, I did plan my journey this way, to have a one-month "holiday," living the Thai island life after five months back-packing through India. Even if my rational mind doesn't think I need recuperation or integration time, my subconscious, heart, and soul have timetables of their own.

First impression of Bangkok: unbelievably clean and well-organized. My system and psyche were taken aback by air conditioning, cell phones, toll plazas, shopping malls, skyscrapers and Skytrains. I didn't sense a Third World bone in Bangkok's infrastructure.

I felt my heart break a little, a sense of sadness in saying goodbye to India—a land where the last thing one needs to bother with is "looking good," or buying this, that, and the other. In India—at least in the circles I moved in—it's natural to look beautiful by the smile in your heart and the way you move through the world. The lack of a "consumer culture" and less consumption choices leaves more room for honest expression; there's more room to focus on the person beneath the facade.

Upon arrival, I was privileged to stay with friends of a friend from France—a married expat couple—in their gorgeous penthouse apartment overlooking the Thai capital city. I sat down carefully on their white upholstered furniture, afraid I might muss something up. I felt absolutely filthy lying on the crisp, clean white sheets. In my first real shower in months, I wondered if my feet would ever get clean. After several scrubbing attempts, I decided to give up and wait until I am back in the States to break out the heavy exfoliation artillery.

The next morning, I ventured out to a proper department store to buy a new bathing suit for the islands, which threw me headfirst in the deep end of the consumer culture pool of buy, buy, BUY (and shop some more while you're at it!). I caught myself standing aimlessly between the Estee Lauder and Chanel counters, staring into space like an Indian milking cow, wondering how one could possibly ever shop in such a store with so many choices.

After spending a full day in Bangkok, it hit me: now I knew how immigrants, refugees, or visitors from undeveloped nations go into absolute shock upon arrival to the U.S. It's paralyzing. When your whole life is based around a much, much simpler model, your frame of reference is simpler as well. Arriving in the West, it's got to be a sudden onslaught of overkill: too much to choose from—sensory overload and confusion. It's got to take a long, long while for eastern foreigners to integrate—if they are ever able to. And now I understand why immigrants from undeveloped nations tend to stick together in little Chinatowns, or other such ethnic communities. There, the world just makes more sense.

After wandering around the department store and soaking up the air conditioning, I finally found the proper "Ladies Wear" floor and bought my bikini. I told myself I needed to switch gears and stop all this useless pining for chai and chapati; it was time to get to an island and have a holiday. And besides, Bangkok was hotter than hell, and simply unbearable without a surf to jump into.

Island Girl

16ᵗʰof April, Koh Phangan

Life is good at the moment. I find myself on the island of Koh Phan-gan in the Gulf of Siam. Turquoise waters, white sandy beaches, palm trees. Daily Thai massages with a lot of muscle that simultaneously pro-vide a chiropractic adjustment. Pineapple-mango-papaya shakes, and *padh Thai* noodles with lots of peanuts and lime. *Oh yeah.*

Most travelers I'd talked to warned me about this island—full of cra-zies and too much loud dance music (it's the island most famous for its Full Moon Party extravaganzas)—but I've rarely been one to heed the opinions of others. A backpacker island appealed to me, anyway. I needed someplace cheap, with diversity and interesting freaky folks to befriend. And, of course, the option to dance: besides my brief time in Goa, I've had a serious deprivation of dancing in conservative India.

It took me a while to get my sea legs on this island. The average travel-er here must be about 22, and it's a whole different backpacker ballgame in Thailand than in India. I can't say it entirely suits my fancy, yet I've definitely made the most of it, filling my soul with tourist fun and sun. After a couple of false starts, I finally found a bungalow on the quiet, western side of the cape of a beach area called Hat Rin. At my little nest, Poseidon's Cove, I sit on my terrace and watch the most beautiful sun-sets—it feels like a different island from the "sunrise" party side.

Turns out, I am paying unexpected homage to my yoga teacher, Anil, here on this little island. The first evening I arrived, I met a very tall, corkscrew curly-haired Swiss woman by the name of Chantal, and we shared a meal. After we ate, though it was quite early, I excused myself and explained that I had to get up early the next morning before the scorching heat in order to get back on track with yoga. Chantal immediately asked if I would teach her, as she'd never done yoga before and was quite eager to learn. "Of course!" I replied.

Chantal was definitely motivated, and adjusted her leisurely holiday schedule to meet me at 7:30 a.m. under the palm trees (out of the way of falling coconuts—apparently one of the major causes of tourist deaths in Thailand—really!).

Another gal, Sylvia from Austria, had also joined our evening dinner conversation, and she wanted to participate as well. That morning, I accidentally blurted out a giggle as she stumbled out of her bungalow, walking across the lawn toward us with the first morning's cigarette dangling from her mouth. Well, perhaps this loud-mouthed American girl had a little bit *too* much of a laugh at her smoky approach to Sun Salutations: we heard that Austrian Sylvia left the island the next morning, never to be seen doing yoga with us again. Oops.

Chantal's apprenticeship was much more successful. Our first yoga lesson turned into a one-week intensive. Together, we got ourselves up with the sun and practiced those moves that Anil had drilled into my mind during the cold Rishikesh winter. I felt such joy and gratitude sharing in Chantal's progress. Chantal had to head back to Switzerland after seven days, yet the smiles stretched across her face were everlasting. After a year of traveling round the world, she said it was the best send-off present she could have ever hoped for.

As they say: "We teach what we need to learn." I am by no means a qualified yoga teacher, let alone a full-on *yogini*; yet, it feels so "right" to be given this gift, and the more I share what Anil taught me, the more it's imprinted in my own being. With each day, the postures become more natural, more of an inseparable part of my daily routine.

Now THAT is the kind of stuff I wanted to bring home from India in my backpack!

Homeward Bound

24th of April, Koh Phangan

I'm heading home a week early! I can feel it—I've come to the end of my journey. For about the last three weeks I've been feeling the itch. It's not that I'm tired or sick, I don't have some weird disease, and there's no anti-American sentiment flying my way.

No, it's none of that. I'm simply *done*—for now. There's only so much sensory input one can absorb in a single trip. Perhaps, with the right mindset, the ending is where the good stuff really begins to kick in! The West is, after all, where you get the lovely opportunity to bring it all "home" (wherever that may be—home being in the heart) and put it into practice.

For me, it's all about integration, and sharing, and using what I've learned and opened up to in the East. That is, at least until I settle in for about five days, dust off my backpack, and find myself looking online for the best ticket deal to the next destination. Ah, will I ever really settle? Regardless, I am excited and grateful to be heading back to California in less than one week's time.

It has been a long haul, and the road has definitely risen up to meet me.

The U.S.A. Today

20th of May, San Francisco

Closure and completion—the culmination of an epic journey is the hardest chapter to write. I've been grieving the end of my travels through India for the past three weeks. It's time to make the transition, to be here now, back in the West. Talking with a compassionate friend over lunch the other day, I tearfully expressed my confusion about being back in the States. He enlightened me, "Erin, you're obviously still ON your trip!"

I've been experiencing my own version of a Mini-Meltdown since arriving in the U.S. The first week flew by and I recovered from jet lag quickly. The second week I discovered that I didn't get off so easy. Friends who have traveled extensively in India had warned me that the return home often greets us with harsh culture shock—in reverse. I wasn't immune. The biggest challenge is facing my resistance to reintegrating in the first place! Part of me has not wanted to be here; I have dreamed of the simplicity and sanctity of my time in India with a fondness that grips my heart and soul.

My second week home, I felt a flood of creative energy rush through me that manifested itself as insomnia. It vibrated like a force field through my body as my spirit struggled to switch frequencies, to slow down the *shakti* vibrations. At first, I resisted the change in resonance—

a shift from a spiritual frequency to a material frequency—but I finally succumbed to it, if only to be able to get some sleep and feel more comfortable in this western land. I was afraid to give in to the shift, to allow myself to slow the spiritual accelerator. I had to, or I'd suffer from exhaustion, or drive myself mad!

Still, three weeks after landing back in the States, I'm often hit with a sudden surge of emotion. In addition to confusion, my tears have been of immeasurable joy mixed with frustration. How can I possibly convey to you, dear friends, one small iota of the beauty I've experienced through this epic journey?

This must be what an artist grapples with as she embraces her creative process, as she struggles to paint her raw vision on the canvas. All I can do is try, and hope to convey a small feeling, a tiny fraction of my enormous Technicolor experience, as well as the boundless gratitude overflowing from my heart.

I've often felt like fleeing since arriving back in California. Of course, it's good to be here, hug my mom, kiss the cat, take a real tub bath. Yet, I feel like a foreigner in my own land. The desire to return to India for another six months, or one year, is still with me. I've thought about going back—this time listening more closely to the secrets She only began to reveal to me. I've ruminated over the idea of writing a book while being in India for another long stint. I've dreamed about letting this paradoxically rich and impoverished jewel of a nation deepen its effect on me.

I'm debating whether to wear my trademark bindi on a regular basis. Seems even the progressive northern California natives aren't quite sure what to make of it. It's funny, because I forget the jewel is sticking out in the middle of my forehead half the time. This past weekend, I came out of a grocery store and asked a middle-aged, conservatively dressed woman for directions to the freeway. She responded to me with a cocked head and a cautious voice, avoiding my eyes. As she was giving me directions, I wondered why she seemed so uncomfortable speaking to me—I'm quite a friendly extrovert, and strangers are usually happy to

converse with me. As I walked away, I realized that she had been staring (or, rather, trying not to) at the pink bejeweled bindi blaring out
of my forehead! I suppose she feared I might do some sort of Vulcan
mind-meld on her, whisk her off to India, and shave her head if she got
too close. *Interesting,* I realized, *this is what it feels like to look exotically
foreign*—and that's mild!

It was at another supermarket where I fully realized I was 100% back
in the U.S.A. Five days after I landed, I finally ventured out on my own
to buy a few staples. After 45 minutes of pulling the glazed-eye-Indian-
milking-cow bit, wandering up and down the aisles and coming up with
just two items for purchase, I was wiped out from sensory overload. I
mean, come on, now. How many types of breakfast cereal must there be?

I ambled over to the checkout line with my two items, stood there, and
overheard the following:

Checkout Lady: "Oh! You found it! Isn't it just wonderful?!"

Shopper Lady: " I don't know yet! But I saw it and just HAD to try it!"

Checkout Lady: "You will just LOVE it. I don't know how I lived
without it! It's so ingenious! Just stick it on and go! It's…GRILLABLE
CHEESE!"

I had traveled 10,000 miles to get back home in order to experience
the Eighth Wonder of the World: modified flavored plastic that won't
burn up on the BBQ.

There are magical moments of homecoming and remembrance, too.
This past weekend, a relative stranger who heard about my voyage asked
me a powerful question. He didn't pull the old, "How was it?" nor did he
ask, "What was your favorite place?" He thoughtfully enquired, "What is
one of your most poignant memories of being in India?"

I burst into tears. I knew immediately. As he listened intently and with
compassion, I described the most incredible peace I've known, meditating at sunset on the Indian Ocean on my little stretch of beach paradise.
Every evening, no matter where the day had led me, I knew right where

I would be come those final minutes of sundown. I'd make a beeline for the beach, spread my sarong out before the surf, and time it just right.

After thirty minutes or so of silent contemplation, I'd open my eyes just in time to see the big ball of orange fire fall off the edge of the Earth and disappear over the horizon. Sometimes at this moment, I'd glimpse a faint white light surrounding my body. Bowing to the setting sun in a *Namaste* prayer position, I'd give thanks for the Sun, that incredible source of *pranic* life energy.

"See you tomorrow!" I'd say, as I waved goodbye to the Sun for another good night.

And that is, quite simply, as good as it gets.

And on that note, I'll wave goodbye to *you*—for this trip, for now.

INTERLUDE
India Calling

Upon returning to the U.S. after my first journey through India, I was so disoriented, so cracked-open and so naturally *high* that for weeks I told anyone who'd listen:

"It's like I've had a lobotomy, but it's only half-complete. I need to go back to India to finish the job."

I grieved every single day that summer, missing the elixir of love and soul and freedom of spirit I'd discovered in India. Finally, fearing I'd never come down off my spiritual high, I consulted a transpersonal psychologist. I needed help, it seemed, for I was in the midst of some sort of "spiritual emergency." Lucky for me, this therapist completely validated my state and my heart's longing, encouraging me to return to India, for clearly, I'd left my heart on Her soil. I began to make plans for an autumn return.

But a funny thing happened on my way to the travel agent, and I spent the next three years stuck stateside, seemingly to get all my remaining ya-ya's out: a desire arose—*just one more plunge into the material side of life*, I thought. I also had nagging doubts that I was truly sane—perhaps I qualified for the loony bin with all this "India Intoxication." Perhaps, instead of taking off, I better stick around the U.S., work hard, and focus on saving for retirement like a good girl.

With the best of intentions to "settle down," I attended grad school and promptly dropped out after the first semester: sitting in a classroom to learn about the world seemed like an insult when I knew that the world was my greatest teacher. I dabbled in theater, discovering that I had no real acting talent and the only character I play flawlessly is my own self. Instead, I tapped into my writing and stargazing skills, and spent the next two years writing content for a top international astrology website.

All during this wild Western ride, I pined for the East and Mother India every day. Seeing documentaries in local art house cinemas on wandering sadhus, or the Kumbh Mela, or the gypsies of Rajasthan, did nothing to assuage my heartache. I told myself I should be happy—once again, I had it all: I lived in one of the world's most gorgeous cities, had a creative and unique career, and a ton of talented, loving friends.

But no. The lobotomy wasn't finished. I couldn't resist the pull back to India, and a fast-paced life in the States still felt like a burden, a weight on my chest.

Once again, I said sayonara. After a blowout bon-voyage bash, I loaded up my backpack, and gave away 99% of everything I had acquired. A coworker who was short on cash and had just relocated from Texas was pleased as punch when I offered her my *entire* apartment of furnishings—pots, pans, TV and DVD, bed, linens—everything but the kitchen sink, for whatever amount she could afford. "It's just *stuff*," I reminded myself as I deposited her $150.00 check. "One can always get more *stuff*."

The return to India had been three long years in coming, and *oh*, how I was ready…

PART TWO
Diving Deeper

Terra Incognita

22nd of September, San Francisco

Today, I paid for my (gasp!) one-way ticket back to India, with a brief stop in Thailand, departing in three week's time. Don't know how long I'll be gone for. Wearing sketched plans like a loosely-draped sarong.

I've been aching to return to the mothership ever since I crash-landed back in California three-and-a-half years ago. It's been a long haul, waiting it out in the West: a stint in Manhattan, a gig at the daily grind, a spurt on the stage, a splash on the page...I've paid my U.S. dues. It's time to be refueled, nourished, and held in the heartland.

Terra incognita, indeed.

Same, Same—But Different

25th of October, Bangkok

"Same, same... but different."

It's a saying travelers hear all the time throughout Southeast Asia and India, a simplified international phrase used by the locals to describe just about anything. It means, "We're getting close to nailing down what we're really describing (a menu item, a bus route, a guest house room)." Even though it's not *quite* what you're after exactly, you'll be pleased enough with the results.

Same, same... but WAY different. That's the way I feel about Thailand this time around. Three-and-a-half years ago, after being in India for such a long stretch, I'd experienced quite a culture shock here. At that time, Thailand felt like the West. Now, I am convinced that it *is* the West. In three years, globalization has taken hold in a huge way.

When I got here two weeks ago, I was blown away at the change in Bangkok—cell phones, Blackberries, Starbucks, sophisticated Skytrains. Bangkok has evolved into a truly modern city. Is this a good thing? I'm not sure, but I have to remember that it takes a good chunk of time to get one's traveling "sea legs." I feel a bit shaky at the moment—a bit rusty.

After two days in Bangkok, I caught a domestic transfer flight to the south of Thailand to get some beach time before heading to the hot, sweaty, dirty north of India. I returned to Koh Phangan, the famed back-packer island. I knew it would be cheap, and easy to meet fellow travel-ers. A good place to chill out, and socialize as desired.

The first change that surprised me is that prices in Thailand had dou-bled over the last three years. But the real shock was the development on the island itself. I should have known this was coming, as heavy-duty construction had begun during my previous trip. Still, when I walked up to my old beach bungalow, Poseidon's Cove, I could have cried at the sight. Before, there were several simple, charming wooden shacks with verandas facing the sunset sea. Now, Poseidon's was one big square con-crete slab. No view. No open grassy area under the coconut trees where I once practiced morning sun salutations. Just a two-storied plot of rooms that looked like a penitentiary block. You could be *Anywhere*.

My heart broke. I entered the premises, just for the heck of it, to say hello and see what the vibe would be. I immediately recognized the Thai owner.

He was sitting behind the front desk, watching TV. "*Sa-wat-dee-ka!*" I greeted him with a big smile, trying to be polite in my non-existent Thai. "Hello! I remember you from three years ago! You are owner, with family!"

"Yes, yes, that long time ago," he replied. "Much changed now." Was it my imagination, or did he not seem as happy now, even with his "il-lustrious," prosperous hotel expansion? It seemed he lacked the warm twinkle in his eyes from before.

The room rates were double the old price (400 Baht—about $9.50). Of course, the owner explained, I would have A/C and TV, and flushing toilet. Not my cup of Nescafe, thank you very much. There's no way I could stay here, nor did I choose to afford it.

Before leaving the grounds, I walked around a bit, trying to scope out an entrance to the sea. There used to be a lovely grassy central area opening up to a grove of coconut trees and the beach, where I loved to practice yoga in the mornings and watch the children play at sundown. No more.

I scurried off as tears actually welled up in my eyes, determined to skedaddle further up the coastline and find a little piece of peace. Off I trod, squish-squashing in my flip-flops through the slurping sand as a light rain fell upon me and all my belongings. I had marveled at the über-organized Germans on the ferry to the island as they oh-so-practically and preparedly covered their rucksacks with some special, handy-dandy fitted canvas coverings that had somehow evolved in backpacker gear repertoire over the past few years. Oh well, you can't think of everything. That wouldn't be adventurous, now would it?

I romped aside millipedes and through mud puddles up the jungly coastal trail. Finally, three bungalow compounds later, I came into a clearing of open space and a humble villa. Jutting up against the forest, fragrant, colorful flowers everywhere, the sea lapping up against the land, on the veranda perched a squat, smiling, older Thai man with his young wife and small child. Could it be the authentic place I was searching for?

"Bungalow?" I asked hopefully.

"One only!" he responded with a grin. "Single, fan only, toilet outside! 100 Baht."

Now that's more like it! I inspected the digs first, as I always do, but my gut had known immediately it was the place for me. "I'll take it!" I told the old man. I would have paid double that price just for the lovely essence of the place. I thanked my lucky stars that these little hovels have survived, even in an overdeveloped island like Koh Phangan. I was so much happier there than in a deluxe resort room. I don't mean to say that I don't appreciate luxury; first class suits me just fine at times. But that's not the type of Asia traveler I wish to be this time around. It's not the point. Plus, I'm in for the long haul, and saving two or three or four dollars a day goes a long, long way.

Exhausted, I threw off my pack and flung myself down on the bed, too tired to tuck the mosquito netting in. It had been a hard haul from San

Francisco, via Taipei, through Bangkok as I had made my way down to the island. I was beat, and very much looking forward to a long, sweaty nap.

The cicadas began their cacophony outside in the pre-sunset heat. I tuned them out and fell into a trance, and had just about dozed off when, suddenly, I became Little Miss Muffet.

Half- asleep, I felt something drop—phwap—onto my left hand. Not wanting to look, but forcing myself, I found myself staring at a big, furry friend—an arachnid, three-inches in diameter.

Welcome to the jungle.

With a loud yelp, I bolted upright and flung the tarantula look-alike into a corner of the hut. Inspecting the room for more spiders, telling myself there was nothing to worry about and it was right-quick time to toughen up, young lady, I finally drifted off to sleep—after coating myself with ultra-toxic DEET (screw citronella—it's no time for au natural in the tropics!) and, this time, triple-checking the net was securely tucked in.

Sometime in the middle of the night, a complete chorus of brass horns started blowing somewhere in the jungle, just behind my bungalow. *That's odd. I wonder who's up and playing jazz in the middle of the night?* I got up, making my way to the outside toilet with the moon as my guide, and looked and looked around the bungalows behind mine. No lights on, nobody home. No one blowing horns and no wayfaring trippers still up with iPods blaring. I shrugged, jetlagged and out of it, and tumbled back to bed. I tightly screwed in my earplugs, figuring I'd investigate in the morning.

The next evening, sometime after supper, I was heading back from the village through the jungle path, when I heard the horns again. This time, smartly outfitted with headlamp, I followed the sound. Determined, I bushwhacked through the palm trees into the next resort, sidestepping the swampy drainage ditches. The sound got louder and I knew my suspicions must be true. I shined the headlamp into the murky depths of a stagnant slough, and there they were! A veritable saxophone symphony, a righteous convention of amphibious musicians! All shapes and sizes of frogs, blowin' their brass like no tomorrow, mimicking Miles and Coltrane in perfect two-four timing!

Now, that's why they call them horn-y toads!

It was a fabulous "welcome back to travel!" granted by Mother Nature Herself. After three days of making miserable comparisons to the way things used to be, I realized that this compare and contrast with the past head-trip had to stop immediately. Otherwise, there'd be no way I'd enjoy any part of Thailand, let alone what changes I might come across in India.

Things change. I've changed. The world is changing—rapidly. Globalization: it's hard to accept. Still, how can I judge the desire of a developing nation to grow, to modernize, to seek comforts of the West? How can I expect them to preserve their traditional ways, staying poor and rudimentary just for my sake? It's a complex issue, one I am sure I will be forced to confront throughout my journey.

To be sure, the comparison trip can be a real devil when traveling, especially upon returning to a place you've visited before. I suppose one way I can bypass this trickster to some extent is to go to new places as much as possible. Certainly, that's got its pluses and minuses as well— part of the draw to return to India is to revisit some of the spots that I consider "home," at least spiritually. We shall see.

All things considered, I dare say: if you haven't yet traveled to the East, and feel the call:

Go. Now.

Jai Maa Kali

27th of October, New Delhi

Oh me, oh my. Where to begin? My heart is simply *bursting* with joy. I have landed, with grace, back in India. The essence of the Divine Mother seeps from every pore of the nation. The arms of this country embrace me truly, as if I were a child returning home after an overly long absence. The energy is powerful. I feel *love* in indescribable ways.

Instantly upon arrival at Indira Gandhi International Airport, I knew I was on the right track in each and every way, as I guided three frightened young women travelers to share my prearranged awaiting taxi. Coming straight from the beaches of Thailand themselves, and it being their first time in India, they were understandably intimidated at the prospect of finding rooms and navigating the chaos upon landing late at night in Delhi.

As these young women—one from Beijing, two from Brazil—approached me at the customs exit (did I have a look that said "old India hand" written on my face?), I took them under my wing: "No worries, girls. Now cover up those spaghetti straps with some clothing, and follow me into the dirtiest, craziest, most wonderful, beautiful slurry of activity—the Main Bazaar of Pahar Ganj—and we'll get you some rooms."

I explained to the prearranged taxi coordinator that he would have to fit all four of us, bags and all. Of course he had no problem, no problem at all, when he learned there was an extra 300 rupees in the pot for him.

And, to my sheer GLEE, as the minivan taxi pulled up next to us curbside, on the windshield was a huge banner decal stating "JAI MAA KALI."

Maa Kali is the fierce goddess that watches my back. An incarnation of the ultimate Mother, Kali is the divine slayer of illusion, and a great protector and source of guidance for me. Of course She would be the chosen guardian of my very first Indian transport-chariot! Perfect. My heart sang, as I spontaneously repeated the words aloud, with gusto, into the hazy Delhi night, "Jai Maa Kali!"

Surprised, the taxi man turned to look at me, a foreign girl who'd just joyfully sent a prayer to the heavens aloud. But the Indian didn't miss a beat; with a great white, toothy grin beaming from his beautiful brown face, he repeated after me:

"Jai Maa Kali!"

And off we went, a group of girls piled into the minicab, braving the INSANE driving behavior of India, whirling into the dusty, sparkling, chaotic, colorful, fantastic adventures that India—and Maa Kali—has in store.

Natural Woman

28th of October, New Delhi

Here, in the capital of the nation, I made a family of friends before I even unzipped my bag.

Last night, at the rooftop restaurant of our hotel, I sat drinking chai after chai for hours with a cavalcade of travelers—English, Dutch, American, French, Palestinian, Swiss, Italian, Japanese, Chinese, and Israeli. Along the way, someone discovered that I love to sing.

And I do love to sing. I do, I do! So, at their prodding and gentle encouragement, I serenaded the dark, smoky skies of Delhi, as a few leftover fireworks from the recent Diwali holiday exploded into the inky night. A complete *a cappella* rendition of Carole King's "Natural Woman"(made famous by Aretha Franklin of course) spilled forth from my soul. Almost effortless, it was as if the muse of India Herself coaxed and coddled the song from my heart, from my core. Even as I was singing, with the requisite multi-accented backup team on chorus, there wasn't a shred of self-consciousness. None at all. Rather, it was the most natural feeling in the whole, wide, glorious world.

Today, a group of us are off for a whirlwind of fun in the bazaars of Old Delhi—the tiny, mazelike streets of Chandi Chowk and the Thieves Market. And tonight, I head east via bus to Pushkar, for the Camel Fair, in the deserts of Rajasthan.

Indian Dream

30th of October, Pushkar

Even after a jolting, jarring, fifteen-hour tourist bus ride to Pushkar, Rajasthan—a journey that takes less than five hours by car, I still can't peel the smile off my face. My perma-grin reveals: "I'm so grateful to be here. I'm so happy to be "home" again, a part of this global family."

The past days, I've been exploring the hustle and bustle of trading camels, horses, and dust of the Camel Fair. I've also been "adopted" by a tailor's family living along the ghats of Brahma's holy lake—laughing with the kids, eating *chapati, dal,* and *subji* on the floor, receiving beautiful henna tattoos on my hands. Evenings, I'd hike up the hill to watch the sunset from the sacred Saraswati temple.

And—*Ram Ram Jaya Ram*—I was given an Indian name by a Hindu priest called Maharaji Shiva. It was at an evening *puja* on the holy lake. I was minding my own business, watching the Full Moon ceremonies, when a white-clad priest, who was clearly after donations, offered to give me an Indian name. Sure, I thought. Why not? Randomness is as good as anything.

Swami pulled pen and name out of a hat and wrote it down in my notebook: *Sapna.* I laughed and laughed when he told me the meaning: DREAM. "Nice, *Ji.* I'll go with that," I said as I gave him a big smile and fifty rupees for his creativity. Yes, that's me—just plain *dream*-y.

"Sapna" is much easier for the locals to remember than "Erin," and the Hindi name brings a smile to their faces. "Mera naam Sapna hai!" I say. *My name is Sapna*

"Sapna! Good name!" they respond, with an exaggerated, head-wobbling nod of approval.

As if to remind me of the perfection of the cosmos, the next morning I received emails from two separate friends back in the U.S. relaying in-depth dreams they'd had that night about me, in India.

Sapna. A dream traveler. Walking through the Indian dreamtime.

Gypsies, Tramps, and Thieves

31st of October, Pushkar

I am sitting in Bedouin-style desert tent with a tribal family, some-where in the middle of the vast Camel Fair trading zone. The young gyp-sy daughter whom I met at the edge of the grounds has led me here, to her family's abode. I know she's eventually going to hit me up for money, but I'm willing to deal with it in exchange for indulging curiosity.

Inside the tent, the girl's old father and teenage brother play region-al instruments made of bamboo, coconut, and horsetail hair, and the daughter sings for me in local Rajasthani language. It's more of a wail than a melodic pleasure, but I don't mind. I thank them for the song.

Poorer than dirt, this family offers me all they can—steaming chai from their eternal fire. The mother—who hasn't moved from her squat-ting position the entire time I've been there—reaches through the smoke to give me the tea with leathery, hardworking hands. As I prepare to take the first sip, the old man begins coughing vociferously, hacking up a lung. I pause with the clay tea cup just before my lips. With yellowing eyes, the old man reaches under a dirty blanket and pulls out a brown bottle of unidentifiable substance, followed by a crumpled paper. He hands it to me. I read that the nondescript bottle is medicine. The typed statement, in English, indicates he is being treated for tuberculosis.

The scam is clear: *Money for medicine, madame?* I'm sorry, I can't drink TB-ridden tea, even if it is a ploy. I quickly pantomime that I have a stomach ache, and politely ask that the wife instead please drink the chai she has just gifted me.

I'm a hard-core traveler, but not sure I want to push it, even if I am in *Push*kar. And I am off like a herd of camels.

Here, during festival time, everyone is a friend, and everyone is a con. It's fair time, and tourists are "fair game." As long as you keep in mind that you're constantly being eyed as a "walking wallet," you'll be fine.

Sab Kuch Milega

8th of November, New Delhi

Faster than the speed of enlightenment, my world is changing.

Post-Pushkar camel chaos, I made a much needed "meditation tune-up" pause in Jaipur. After three days of blessed silence in a short Vipassana course, I've returned to the righteous urban rubble, the megacity mayhem of Delhi. *Sab kuch milega.*

"Sab kuch milega"—you'll hear this Hindi phrase thrown around everywhere on the subcontinent. Translation: "Everything is available." Backpackers like to think of it as "everything is possible," for indeed, in India, that is a truism—and it's likely that everything is possible *all at the same time.*

For example: You're stuck in a sputtering, hiccupping local bus in a smoggy traffic jam in the outskirts of Delhi. You peer out the open window, and chuckle to witness a holy man with a flowing white beard and a loincloth zip past your nose on the back of an Enfield motorcycle. Meanwhile the Rajasthani tribal woman a few seats behind you has been shamelessly upchucking a foul, yellow-green fluid substance out the side window for the last ten minutes. Before you even have the chance to consider feeling repulsed, a school bus in the next lane cozies up to your own carriage. Dozens of smiling, laughing children hang half their little bodies out the windows, ecstatically scream *"H-i-i-i-i-i!"* and wave fervently at you, the charmed Westerner. Their sweet little arms stretch toward your lane as they strive to skim fingers with you, instantly giving you that special "Rock Star Glow" of recognition that comes every other moment while Doing the India Dance.

And that's how India is. She turns you on your ear to accept a mixed-up, magical melting pot of life's follies and quirks as part and parcel of the ineffable beauty of life.

Sab kuch milega. Hallelujah.

Doin' Delhi Time (DDT)

9ᵗʰ of November, New Delhi

Sitting in my favorite little hole-in-the-wall café in the Main Bazaar off the New Delhi Train Station, having just ordered a supper of *aloo gobi*, *biryani*, and *paneer*, I gaze out the open storefront entrance, try to shake off the flurry of another ever-hectic Delhi day, and take a deep breath.

As deep as is possible, that is, with the usual mass of carbon monoxide, stench, and excrement in the air. *Ah, well, maybe I should do like the others in here and light up a cigarette to calibrate my lungs*, I sardonically consider as I welcome a particularly fragrant gust of *Eau d' Pollutante*.

The sweet thirteen-year-old waiter boy is about to take my order up to the kitchen, when he stops in his tracks and looks out the front entrance with a look of panic. The sound of a monster machine rumbling down the alley fills the air. *That must be one big-ass truck*, I ponder, *to rise above the relentless, ear-splitting din that is Delhi*. You know something wicked this-a-way comes when a local boy is flustered.

The object of his concern makes its way into my field of vision. Through the tight lane corridor packed with cows, vendors, rickshaws, chai wallahs, fruit stands, and flustered travelers, comes the threatening truck: a chemical tanker, bullying its way through the Pahar Ganj maze, spewing fumy, smoky substance directly into the doors of all the shops, straight into everyone's face. Within seconds, the entire marketplace, including the café where I sit, is overtaken with the white, powdery chemical dust.

Hack, hack. Wheeze, wheeze. Watering eyes... I'm wondering if perhaps some terrorist group has gassed the entire area. "What *is* that, *ji*?" I inquire of the wait-boy, who is still standing there with a wide-eyed look of concern.

"OOH!" he spits out. "Bad! Very bad, madame! It for—you know...!" He makes little pinching motions on his forearm. "In skin! To kill mosquito! Really bad!"

As the chemical wafts all around us, settling onto my hair, skin, and cafe table, I realize what's happened. *Oh. Shit.* Yes, it's confirmed by the well-informed German traveler seated next to me: It's the villainous, toxic DDT.

DDT—DichloroDiphenylTrichloroethane—has been banned in the U.S., but not in India and many other developing nations who rely on the cheap toxin to battle malaria. Proven highly carcinogenic to humans and wildlife, we have been blatantly, shamelessly gassed with the stuff.

Now, do I say, "Oh goodie! Now we will certainly be freed of the risk of highly infectious, mosquito-borne dengue fever!"? Or, rather, what actually spilled forth:

"Fuck. I hope I can still have children."

Yep. Definitely time for a cigarette.

Happenin' at the Hare Krishna

9th of November, New Delhi

DDT gassings aside, life is quite delectable in the Delhi-catessen, with a smorgasbord of delights on offer. Since I've likely left a sticky, sad taste in your mouth from ranting about chemical warfare, perhaps it's necessary to offer a morsel or two of goodness to clear the palate.

In spite of its seeming intimidation, for me, the congested capital of Delhi is relatively manageable. Pahar Ganj, a market area next to the New Delhi Railway Station, is a bustling backpacker *centrale*, with all the necessary resources for travelers—one primary fuel being other vagabonds themselves. My days of late have revolved around the Hare Krishna Guest House, having reconnected with some of the long-term residents I met upon arrival at the end of last month. We seem to have formed a homey "boarding house" atmosphere. A veritable family of lovable freaks—*et mais oui, moi inclus!*

I could spend all afternoon blabbing about effervescent Abhishek, my new Indian "cousin-brother" who is the center of activity—literally— here at the Krishna. Abhishek lives here. Right in the heart of the Hare, the center room on the center floor of the hotel.

Abhishek is a freelance trainer for call centers in the region. He can't stop singing "Love is a Rose," the song I taught him the first night we met. He's determined to teach this song to the customer service reps with great gusto.

"Love is a Rose" *à la* Neil Young may now be the passage to correct consonant pronunciation in offshored industries. The next time you call Dell Computers Customer Service, your India-based representative may have been trained in proper American English through this little ditty of a tune exported by Yours Truly.

The Hare Krishna Crew includes a bevy of other heavies, like "Shushu-Meeta" from Angola. Meeta is "friend" in Sanskrit, as Shushu offhandedly mentioned one full moon night of music on the rooftop. We all loved the phrase so much that Shushu-Meeta became his name, which perfectly suited his ever-present, glimmering display of pearly whites offset against gorgeous chocolate skin.

Shushu-Meeta is seriously into his *bhakti* practice of devotional love for his guru, Satya Sai Baba. He spontaneously plunges into *puja* prayer and song with great fervor, whenever his heart center is exploding with divine love. Shushu strums the same two guitar chords, over and over and over again, wailing heartfelt songs to his God. Loudly. At any time of day, or night.

It's all good. Except for the small detail that he is my immediate next-door neighbor. Apparently, *I* am also meant to be up and a-praying, whether it be 1:00 a.m. or 7:00 a.m.—or both.

Throwing the pillow over my head yesterday morn, a thick Aussie male voice called through the paper-thin floorboards, perfectly in time with Shushu-Meeta's warbling wail and the only two notes repeated, over and over, on the guitar. A call and response ensued:

Shushu-Meeta: "Ba-baaaaaa! Oh, Ba-baaaaa!"

Aussie: "Shut uppppp! Oh, Shut uppppp!"

Repeating, until finally:

Aussie: "WE ARE TRYING TO HAVE SEX!"

Like that. Just another fine morning at the Hare home, overflowing with divine nectar. Who would put a stop to such glorious madness?

Of course, we have the requisite Hare Krishnas staying here. Why, what other hotel could they possibly choose? This is fine with me, as

Krishna energy (divine bliss, song, dance, *bhakti* love and devotion) is definitely welcome in my om.

It's where the heart is, after all.

At the Foot of the Goddess

11th of November, Rishikesh

I arrive at last in Rishikesh, known as the ancient home of traditional yoga, lying nestled at the foot of the Himalayas where the holy Ganges runs clean, clear, and cold. Here, one can romp and roam at the feet of the Goddess herself, the great Ganga Maa. Her waters are turquoise and clear, her sands are white and smooth. She gives life to India, and she replenishes my soul.

Long before California's power yoginis cut DVD's and late-night Infomercials, this relatively quiet enclave of temples and ashrams hosted sincere seekers, giving devotees the spiritual sustenance of Vedanta philosophy as well as hatha asana.

Rishikesh is one of my spiritual homes here in the motherland. Perhaps it's the wannabe rock star in me that is attracted to the old base of Maharishi Maresh Yogi, the Beatles' guru. Dilapidated and abandoned, the Maharishi ashram on the Ganges' right bank still carries powerful vibrations in its underground meditation cells, where the Fab Four opened their third eyes and caught aural inspiration for *The White Album*. But we'll get to that tomorrow.

Scampering along the riverbank with a Dutch friend named Gerrald, we are summoned by a chorus of "hellos" and happy young faces. It's a group of children motioning us over to their tiny abode. In this simple mud and dirt home, built into the side of the mountain, live a family of four jubilant sisters and their aging parents.

I greet them in their native tongue: "Apa kaise hai?" *How are you?* They take great delight at the foreigner's weak attempt at Hindi, and the fact that my *"nam"* is Sapna. The girls promptly nickname Gerrald "Jaro," which I suppose is much easier for Indian ears.

I perch on a large boulder in the middle of what appears to be their multipurpose, combination front and back yard, foyer (place to welcome visitors), laundry room (mom is scrubbing on the washboard), kitchen (a pot is boiling on the smoking campfire), and parking garage (a few cows are at the gate).

The two youngest daughters scramble up on the boulder, crawl on my lap, hold my hands, caress my arms, and hug me tight. Running through the back of my mind is the question, "When is the shoe going to drop? When will the *chai-chapati* money be asked for? The school pen requested? The bit of chocolate? The hundred rupees for the family's education, medication, or edification?"

But these questions can be temporarily ignored and then gracefully dealt with as need be. For now, we are having a gay old time.

The slightly interested, graying father peers out the mud hut door, stretching his neck from behind his foot-pedal sewing machine. Perched nearby on the ground, the toothless and happy mother looks on as she scrubs socks and sundries within arms reach of the smoking outdoor fire.

After spending a few laughter-filled minutes teaching the sisters how to play "Patty Cake, Patty Cake," I look up to welcome the middle daughter, Sunita, who has just ran home from school and is now quite breathless and excited to realize that two *very* tall, very white foreigners have descended upon her home.

Sunita is wearing a tiny *bindi* on her golden-brown forehead, nicely offsetting her generous smile and perfectly pressed school uniform. I'm impressed to see that the family is investing in this daughter's education, for their living conditions indicate that they have zero disposable income.

As the little green bindi gem between Sunita's eyes glimmers with the flash of the fading daylight, I suddenly realize that I am myself—gasp—bindi-less.

In weak Hindi, I explain that "Sapna" has a nickname in the U.S., and it's "Bindi Girl."

"YES! *Nam* Bindi Girl! YOU are Bindi Girl! Sunita declares with delightful squeals. Apparently, she likes the idea wholeheartedly. She instantly dashes inside the hut, and comes out with a sheet of bejeweled bindis.

For shame! Bindi could be blind without her blessed beauty mark, third-eye of intuitive wisdom, where "X marks the spot." It's a forehead-feeding frenzy as all the girls gather 'round for proper placement and encouragement, and I am properly anointed.

I can see clearly now.

Maa Durga and the Tiger

14th of November, Rishikesh

Tiger, tiger, burning bright
In the forests of the night,
What immortal hand or eye
Dare frame thy fearful symmetry?
~William Blake

Ever come face to face with a goddess? It's time to meet Maa Durga, who rides a tiger.

Durga, in Sanskrit, means "She who is incomprehensible or difficult to reach." Maa Durga, also known as Jagatambe or Mother of the World, manifests in many forms, including Parvati, the devoted wife of Shiva and mother of the elephant-headed Ganesha. Durga is also the ground of Maa Kali, her most wrathful form. Kali sprang from Durga's forehead to conquer the demons of illusion and suffering.

In India, the veil between worlds is very thin, and the common saying amongst travelers, "everything is possible," is a truism. Through a most unpredictable series of events, I have come to realize directly the nature of the wrathful goddess.

Yesterday, an Australian travel writer, Christine, and I took a walk to the old "Beatles Ashram" near the banks of the Ganga here in Rishikesh.

The dilapidated Maharishi Maresh Yogi center, prior home to the Fab Four's temporary guru, is nestled up against the jungle, at the outskirts of Swargashram at Ram Jhula. I was especially excited about our excursion: I plan on buying a guitar on this trip, and I wanted to offer up rock 'n' roll prayers to give me an extra boost of musical oomph. Little did I know, more than an oomph was on the way on that fateful day of the *lila*, the gods' divine play...

After weaving our way along the Ganga, past flocks of schoolchildren, *chillum*-smoking sadhus, and Hanuman temples, Christine and I arrive at the entrance of the old ashram. The imposing main gate is locked, and a squat, unhappy-looking Indian is scowling at us through the bars. I see the sign: NO ENTRY. *Strange*, I think. *Last time I was here, anyone could come and go as they pleased.*

Well, sister, it's four years later, and The Indian Mafia has arrived.

"Baksheesh!" the pudgy, mustachioed character shouts, like an angry guard at the gates of Oz, demanding bribery money for entry into the gates of pop culture memorabilia. "No, sir!" I retort. "No money! Ashram free!"

"Hundred rupee! Two hundred rupees!" he demands. I marvel at his increasing-price non-bargaining skills.

"*Nahi*," I decline with a firm "no."

"Fifty!" he shouts.

"Nahi." I'm being stubborn, shaking my head in disagreement. Who wants to pay bribe money to pray?

"Forty!"

"*Das!*" I respond. 10 rupees. Last offer. I'm not budging.

Neither is he. No deal apparently. He gives an angry glare our direction, and stomps off. It's truly like a Indian village version of *The Sopranos*, with our own "Tony the Tiger" head honcho, puffing up his chest and bellowing his script: "I own this tourist trap. Don't even try it, ya big white American broad."

I'm determined to get in; nothing motivates me more than a righteous challenge, for better or for worse. Christine and I scour the edges of the tall stone walls to see if there's an alternate entry, to no avail. The ashram walls are too high; not only that, they're lined with monkeys, and Christine tells me she isn't up for being attacked today. "I already had one monkey jump on me this trip, and it scared the hell out of me. I'm not risking a bite and several shots at the clinic," she says. So we scope out the main gate once again, as the watchman is out of sight.

Our luck is in! We spot a couple of weary Swedes making their exit. The Swedes stop to say hello. I notice they look a little sour when they tell us they were forced to shell out fifty rupees *each* to the angry Indian. We commiserate and they take their leave, but not without me noticing the gate they've exited through has been left slightly ajar—unlocked! And the greedy gatekeeper is nowhere around!

"Come on, *let's go!*" I hiss, feeling like a female Tom Sawyer—up to no good but on an adventure, so who cares? Christine and I hustle through the iron gates quickly. I'm not sure whether to feel shameful or victorious. I know what the watchman is doing is totally illegal—demanding baksheesh at any old price he chooses—but I gotta hand it to him, he's got quite the racket going.

Somehow, Christine and I slip past his watchful eye in one fortunate moment, and off we scurry into the ashram grounds. For the next half hour, we enjoy ourselves thoroughly, ambling through the ruins of stone meditation huts and underground meditation cells. That is, until a village laborer appears seemingly out of nowhere, walking out of the jungle wearing a huge afro of collected banana leaves on his head. The Indian approaches us, and it is clear he is encouraging us to get off the premises. He snarls and makes vicious faces, clawing the air with his hands, to indicate we are in danger if we go much further. "Tiger! Tiger!" he is saying. "Jungle tiger!" There are tigers afoot.

Tigers!?! Christine is more than a little nervous now. "I'm not risking this, man. Did I tell you about the hippo attack in Africa?" Me, I'm feeling a bit ballsy since I've been here before, and I reassure her there are no tigers inside; surely they prefer the sanctity of the outlying jungle.

Yet, the sky is beginning to darken, making things quite spooky, so we make toward the exit. As we descend the pathway leading to the main gate, the angry Mafia Man spots us from his balcony and starts screaming at us, ferociously, in Hindi. He is pissed that we've somehow gotten past his watchful eye, and has absolutely no intention of letting us leave without a battle.

I scamper as fast as I can down the slippery, steep path. I want Christine to get a move on, too, but she's dawdling behind, moving much slower than I, seemingly taking her time. *That's why you got attacked by a hippo, girlfriend,* I think. *Hurry up!* I can see about fifty feet ahead, the gate remains unlocked, but the man is swiftly making his way downstairs.

As I'm skidding along in my flip-flops, out of the corner of my eye, I see him grab a stick! A very BIG stick! "Run, Christine! Run!" I yell. But the man reaches the gate before we do. He's got a key with which he intends to padlock us in. He wants to trap us. And he will NOT let us leave.

And then, I do something you're never supposed to do in India: I lose my cool.

I have no idea what comes over me. I suppose I should just pay him the gosh-darned $2.00 or whatever his price has just risen to, but I have lost my head and am now just plain *pissed* at the principle of the matter. I struggle with him at the gate, trying to prevent him from locking us in by grabbing the key out of his pudgy, sweaty hands. He makes lunging motions toward me with his big stick.

In the background, I hear Christine, the peace-loving Australian, trying to sweetly reason with the bully: "Please sir, let us out. You can't lock us in here." She is not helping things at all; everyone knows you can't win with one teammate talking soft, and the other using physical force.

Meanwhile, I become more and more furious. It's like a scene from one of the *Mahabharata* demon battles, as the ogre and I grapple with the big stick, each attempting to take ownership of the weapon. The insane part is that I'm not feeling one tiny bit afraid. Not at all.

OK, maybe a tiny bit—when it finally crosses my mind that he could have a knife. *Good goddess*, it flashes through my mind, *my mother would just FLIP if she knew what I was up to.* I tower over him in height, but he's got me on girth. Somehow, I feel in my heart that if I really needed to violently defend myself, I could—I've got ample enough adrenalin running through my veins—but of course I don't want it to get to this point.

He's managed to get the gate locked with one hand, while menacing me with his stick in the other, and he's put the key in his trouser pocket. We are held hostage.

He starts to pull away, and I do what I have learned instinctively and have never had to do before: I kick him between the legs. OOMPH, there it is.

Admittedly, it's a half-baked shove of a kick, and I aim for the inner thigh instead of the groin because I don't mean to harm him, just to insult him, really. Plus, I'm wearing flip-flops, and can't do a great deal of damage without losing my balance.

But now, I see the REAL tiger that we were warned about. The man's eyes are blazing, burning, burning bright. He begins to curse me and back away from me, calling me and my mother all sorts of names, brandishing his big baton. I climb up the side of the stone wall, which is now lined with monkeys—mamas and their nursing babies, watching the whole fiasco—and beg Christine to get up there with me, in order to leap over the edge.

"No way, I am *not* getting up there." She's having none of it, as the monkeys are more frightening to her than being locked in the ashram with the madman. So she continues with her technique: sweetly pleading with the man to let us out. "Please sir, you can't lock us in here."

Our captor looks upset, scared, nervous, and, frankly, defeated. I see that he has moved toward the gate once again, and as I am climbing back down from the high stone wall to see if we have a chance to be released, he opens the gate just slightly, and lets Christine—and only Christine—

pass through to the sanctity of the other side.

As I make to dart after her, he shouts, "NAHI! No!" and promptly locks me back in. *Shit. Now what? Trapped behind the gates of the Beatles Ashram forever? What am I, some sort of Rock 'n' Roll Rapunzel?*

I hoist myself to peer over the stone wall, and begin to plead with the babas gliding past on the other side, paying no mind to this worldly fiasco. "Baba? Help me, please? Om namah Shivaya!" *In the name of Shiva!* I call out, as the silent renunciates peacefully glance my way, watching the whole show as if there is nothing odd at all about such divine theater, and walk on by.

In fact, it works, this prayer to the peaceful ones, as my captor has some sort of revelation. Perhaps he doesn't want to be shamed by the holy men for entrapment of a helpless tourist. Or perhaps he thinks *I* am the truly mad one, and *he* doesn't want to be left alone with this crazy woman-banshee, an incarnation of the wrathful goddess Herself. Lord knows what I might be capable of.

The tiger has been pacified. He unlocks the gate. I step through. I am free.

Why was I fearless? Was it ego? Stupidity? Principle, perhaps? I'd like to think that this encounter with Maa Durga and the Tiger is showing me I can take care of myself, if and when I have to. And, if the more ferocious, terrifying form of Kali had to spring from my forehead, to level the monster, I could have handled it.

In fact, it seems that holding a mirror up to this man, by reflecting terror to him in a big way, evoked enough fear in him to make him back off.

Needless to say: lucky for me, lucky for the tiger.

Jai Maa Durga!
May the Divine Mother of the Universe bless you,
watch over you,
and free you from the chains of illusion.

Sapna Meets the Sadhu

17th of November, Rishikesh

Life is but a dream. Certainly, my recent encounter at the Beatles' Ashram was otherworldly enough to prove the saying. Now that I've calmed down after placating wild tigers, I'm back to enjoying the easier side of Waking Life.

Here in Rishikesh, known as Land of the Sages, I am coming to a deeper understanding of the Hindi nickname bestowed upon me in Pushkar. The well-wishing priest, Maharaji Shiva, called me *Sapna*. The name, which means "dream," suits me perfectly. I travel quite a bit in the dreamtime. Since cultivating my Dream Life over the past few years—making dream collages, keeping a dream journal, setting bedtime intentions to remember my dreams—the dreamtime has become as rich and nutritious as Waking Life. Traveling through time and across geographical borders, I have been able to speak with artists and sages, contemporary and historical, in the dreamtime. For this, I am grateful.

Recently, I had the good fortune of befriending a sadhu here in Rishikesh—a baba who helped me dive even deeper into my dream odyssey. In the U.S., I have a wonderful coffee table book, a photographic essay on the sadhus, and whenever I look at it, I feel love and warmth in my heart and mind. If there is such a thing as reincarnation, likely I would have been a sadhu in a past life. Some of the sadhus come down from their high Himalayan outposts for the winter, when the snow traps their meditation caves, and settle in for the cold season in lower-altitude, holy homes such as Rishikesh.

I have often wanted to converse with these *babas* as they go through their daily lives and austerities on the banks of the Ganges; I've been quite cautionary as I am, after all, a woman traveling alone, and such situations require sensitivity. A handful of sadhus enjoy socializing with the Westerners while wintering in Rishikesh. Granted, they are rewarded with constantly flowing chai, chapati, and companionship—a good exchange for all concerned.

My fourth day in Rishikesh, sitting in a café, I came to know "Krishna Giri," which literally translates as "Mountain of Krishna." Krishna Giri Baba is a warm soul, generous and open. Not only that, but his time with travelers has granted him with sufficient English skills, and we have been able to have short, but infinitely useful conversations.

Upon introductions and chatter, I told him my American name was Erin, but that I was given the name Sapna, and he could use that if it were easier for him to remember. Krishna Giri frankly dug that my name was "dream." While we chatted over chai, he absentmindedly played with his black hair like a little child, forming new dreadlocks with his fingers. Amused, I noticed that dangling down from his topknot and over his forehead, the long, squirrelly lock of hair naturally formed the shape of a cobra spouting from his crown.

The cobra-fountain triggered a thought: *Oooh, I should ask Krishna Giri about those snake dreams I've been having.* "Can I ask you about my snake dreams, Baba?"

"Snake dream?" he responded, shaken from his reverie. "Snake dream, big dream!" declared Krishna Giri. "Yes, yes! Go ahead!"

So, I took the opportunity to ask this goodhearted sadhu, steeped in the living schools of mystery and devotion, about a series of dreams I had involving snakes and cobras, which began during my first journey to India:

Big Dream #1 came to me four years ago, shortly after arriving to India the first time. I was in Dharamsala at the base of the Himalayas. In the dream, I encountered a large snake. The snake simply greeted me.

Big Dream #2 came to me a few months later, when I first landed in Rishikesh and greeted the river goddess Ganga. In the dream, a snake came to me, and bit me on the hand. At the time, I described my dream to my dear friend Max from the U.K., who was well informed about such symbols especially as relates to yogic philosophy. Max explained that it was quite auspicious to dream about snakes in general, but to be *bitten* by one in the dream was incredibly powerful, and that I was likely have a very strong spiritual awakening.

Big Dream #3 came to me six months ago, back home in San Francisco, during a period of many months of intense dream work. In this dream, a huge cobra engulfed my entire body as I was seated in a meditative, lotus position. The cobra rose up, up, up behind me until it completely covered my head with its massive hood. I felt all seven chakras in my body—root to crown, color by color—light up in the dream.

Upon hearing the much-simplified description of these three "Big Dreams," Krishna Giri stopped mid-sip into the chai I had ordered for him, and stared straight into my eyes. "Yes!" he declared, his eyes exuding sincerity and importance. "Very good dream." He instructed me to go within and let the dream tell me its message, not to ask others what it meant.

I explained that the dreams felt so powerful that I wasn't sure where to begin: "Sometimes I feel like I need a guide to help me." He responded that I already knew what the dreams mean (which is true), and that I already had the wisdom I needed to uncover more (which is also true). In fact, the dream itself was the carrier of the wisdom. "Dream has answer," Krishna Giri said.

Krishna Giri continued his compact lesson. Often, teachings from sadhus and great sages are wonderful because they are short and sweet— maybe ten sentences at the most—ensuring the message lands easily and effectively on the listener. In choppy but fully-comprehensible English, he told me the tale of how, as a young man in his twenties, he lived quite a traditional life outside of Bombay as the son of a man in the Indian army.

"Always," he explained, "I dream of running into mountains, again and again." Finally, at age 28 (he is now 41), he took sadhu vows from his guru and ran straight to the mountains, high into the Himalayas, forever leaving all constraints of worldly life and burning his past in the *agni* (fire).

Once he heeded the dream, responded to the call, and entered the arms of his true mother (earth) and true father (sky), the dream never returned. "Once message received, dream finish!" declared Krishna Giri triumphantly. And with that, the sadhu's supercharged mini-sermon was finished as well.

Ahh, I thought, *he's right!* I got the message, on more levels than one. Krishna Giri's teaching reinforced the truth that dreams are a powerful form of guidance that mustn't be ignored. If we're still dreaming about something, there's some juice there to be investigated.

Certainly, it confirmed that I have embodied the wonderful gift from the sacred cobra, the *Naga.* I was summoned back to India by the power of Kundalini Shakti, the coiled serpent goddess that lies dormant at the base of the spine. She called, and I returned. The goddess was awakened from Her dream.

The Kama Sutra

20th of November, Rishikesh

Can I rate a short story PG-13? Consider yourself forewarned, or be prepared to blush. In lieu of a whole treatise on that ancient Hindu masterpiece on love, sex and sensuality, *The Kama Sutra*, I think a casual encounter will suffice.

After several overnight bus journeys, cramped train trips, and lack of yoga, my body clearly called for a massage. One day, enjoying a lazy Rishikesh afternoon dipping in the icy-cold Ganga and sunbathing under gorgeous blue skies, I happen upon an Ayurvedic spa along the river. I inquire as to whether someone is available for a "treatment," which is posted as "massage with special oil."

Without missing a beat, the bright-eyed, attractive Indian man in his early twenties behind the desk replies with semi-controlled eagerness, "Only two men staff here giving massage today! No women available now!"

Uh-huh. Yeah. Right. I know what this is all about. I'm on to him. I'm quite sure that women practitioners are around if I insist on taking my rupees elsewhere. But my body is cranky and I am not in the mood to quibble. I've enjoyed the occasional deep-tissue massage from male therapists in the West. And, I received a massage by a quite skilled, respectful male masseur at this very same spa four years prior. So I felt comfortable enough. I decide to roll with it. "Okay," I tell the man at the desk. "I'll take it."

The young man instructs me to enter the massage "room," which is nothing more than a screened-in enclosure with a thin mattress pad and a few blankets folded up on the floor. Peering in, I deem it clean and hygienic enough. So I enter, shortly followed by—yes, you guessed it—the very same, smiling young man from the front desk.

A-ha. Of *course* he is the aforementioned "Man on Staff" today. *Alright, let's see how this goes.*

Isn't it interesting that Indian women masseuses request you leave your knickers on, requiring that you remove only your brassiere, yet the men have different requirements for their technique? After informing me that I need to remove *all*—yes, all—of my clothing and lie face down on the floor, the masseur sets to work.

Monsieur Masseur the Eager knows very well that this is his lucky day and seems to possess no qualms about expressing his glee—his telling grin stretches from ear to ear. Just look at his good fortune: a liberated American woman who will oblige and not balk at his request to remove all of her clothing, for she is accustomed to receiving nude massages in the West.

He begins with a somewhat skillfully delivered "oil treatment," and—well, let us just say—Monsieur Eager takes advantage of the opportunity to treat various parts of my anatomy with excruciating detail. I'm sure that Ayurveda considers the *chest* area to be a very important, sensitive area, requiring much linger and attentiveness, no?

Conscientiously caressing my calves—surely opening up sensitive acupressure points and activating energy meridians, yes?—he delicately removes my silver anklets as attentively as a lover would tend to his consort. *Holy cow shit*, I'm thinking. *What in Shiva's name did I get myself into here?*

Sure, I know I can halt the course of events at any moment I may feel uncomfortable. At this point, however, I'm slightly amused and curious as to how long this pseudo-sexual savant is going to keep up his professional demeanor before he flips a lid.

And then. Flip a lid he does.

All that repressed energy stemming from being raised in a sexually-conservative, arranged-marriage culture spills out. While I'm lying on my back, he torques one coconut oil-basted leg high over my head—a yogic stretch that, believe it or not, is highly beneficial for hip-opening. It's now apparent to the masseur that I am, indeed, quite flexible.

"Very good body, Madame!"

"Oh?" I respond drowsily. I'm quite relaxed, half-asleep and enjoying the manipulation of my much-neglected musculature. But then, suddenly, Monsieur Masseur jumps up and starts tugging at his clothes. *Something* has set him off.

"You having (*gasp*) much power, Madame! I think you having more power than me! *Ho!* So much... so much *Shakti!*" He is actually wailing.

Startled, I pull myself out of my passive posture and raise my head. "I'm sorry?" I mutter.

"Yes! So *hot*. Energy so *hot*. I feel myself... I feel... I'm having to remove my clothing!"

I hope he's not serious. *He's just having his kicks.* On the other hand, for all I know, he could be telling the truth. It's quite likely I do have a lot of energy running through me and, if he is worth his healing salts, he could be absorbing it.

The guy is now sweating profusely and wiping his face with his t-shirt. Before I have time to respond, or grab a sarong to cool things down a bit, he gets back to the task at hand. Walking behind me, he confidently props me up like a rag doll in seated position. Next, he pours a bucket of oil on my head, works the 40-weight into my hair, and vigorously scratches my scalp.

Whatever in the hell he's just done, I'm happy, cured, pleasantly wrecked. *That was fucking great.*

"Now, you have FULL POWER, Madame!" he declares triumphantly.

For an encore, he guides me into an herbal steam bath compartment—
a body-size plywood box compartment with a wooden bench to perch
on—and a space for my Flock-of-Seagulls, Medusa-mopped oily head to
pop out the top.

Masseur plops a wet towel on my head and turns on the sultry steam.
But he plays his fantasy trump card just before he closes the contraption:
"OK, Baby, sit tight," he commands, as if he were Al Pacino ordering his
moll around. Shaken from my dazed state by the inappropriate use of
the word "baby," I contemplate whether to chide his tone. *Whatever*, I
conclude. At this point, I'm mashed potatoes—too hot, cooked, and oily,
to be bothered.

Post-sauna, I shower, change, and take my leave through the lobby. A
group of young men is hanging outside the spa, with glimmering eyes
and expectant ears. I can feel them watching my every move as I pass
them. They're surely about to demand a play-by-play update from Monsieur—my cue to make a particularly quick exit, and off I stride toward
the bridge that will lead me across the river to my own private boudoir.

Minding Mara's Daughters

4th of December, Igatpuri

The Vipassana International Academy in Igatpuri, Maharashtra lies about three hours east of Mumbai, close to the city of Nasik. The meditation center here, called Dhamma Giri, or "mountain of Dharma," is the largest in the world. Every year here, tens of thousands of international participants receive the teachings of Vipassana—the intense form of sitting meditation from the Theravadan Buddhist lineage of Southeast Asia. In fact, during my course, there were to be 222 ladies participating—and that's just the *women!* Therefore, you can imagine how intense the vibrations were—so many people meditating at extreme levels of concentration.

It was to be my fourth foray "going in" to the ten-day meditation depths, with one caveat: this time, I was to be a Dhamma *sevika*—a server working as a volunteer at the course instead of sitting the usual eleven hours a day along with the other students.

Even going in as a "server" volunteer, I felt incredibly insecure. I have a "push-pull" relationship with my sitting practice, which is spotty at best. Usually, I keep my meditation sittings regularly for about two months after a retreat; then, life happens in a big wave, and I lose it. I've given up the guilt over it, though; I know meditation is there for me whenever I need it, and I try to practice the principles of equanimity—keeping a calm and balanced mind—in my everyday life. But still, I absolutely, positively wanted to bail. Walking into this world headquarters of Vipassana was intimidating. The waiting list is usually a mile long to take a course here, and many serious students stay here for months at a time, working diligently. Clearly, I was out of my league.

Upon registration, after receiving my "Dhamma Sevika" name badge, I walked into my assigned rudimentary private room, threw off my grimy pack, and looked around at the space that was to be my home for the next twelve days.

Right away, I sat down on the bed and prayed—which is antithetical to being in a Buddhist meditation center, I well know, but hey, the course hadn't begun yet, and if there's anything that keeps me sane and connected to my Self and the greater Plan of Existence, it's a good, old-fashioned plea to the Ultimate Powers-That-Be. I muttered, *God, I don't think I can do this. I really don't. I'm not going to unpack yet. I think I have to go down to the main office and tell them I've changed my mind. I'm unfit to serve this course. Better I leave now than climbing through the bathroom window on Day Four to skip town, yes? So help me now. I need a sign. Pronto!*

I'd felt this sort of panic before. In the year before I first came to India, while visiting family in Europe, I served a similar three-day meditation course in Belgium. Even though it was my very first time serving on a course, for some strange reason, the teachers assigned me the top-dog job of Female Course *Manager*. I was the person ultimately responsible for all of the women participants. *Great…how did I get to be an example?*

During the Belgian retreat, I almost DID crawl out my bedroom window one night. The women were having the usual meltdowns—wanting to leave, not sure they could continue in silence—and it was my job to help them stay strong and not leave in the middle of the course. I felt like a hypocrite and a failure; but somehow I stuck it out, and so did all of the women. By some small miracle, no one quit that course, not even me.

This is the experience I am remembering as I am praying for the strength to go forward this time. I have severe doubts, but I also know myself to be a courageous person who scarcely backs away from a challenge. I've also sat three long, ten-day courses, and giving back through service is a major part of this tradition. It represents a sort of full-circle completion for me. As they say, we can't keep what we don't give away. I want to be able to give the same opportunity that I have received to the women who are fearlessly surrendering themselves to this meditation technique. Someone gave it to me, and it's my turn. *I can't let them down; I'd be letting myself down, since it's all one big wheel turning 'round.*

So I pull my wits about me, take a shower, and change into my one traditional Indian outfit—a Punjabi suit with loose pants, a shawl, and long top. It is shabby and worn from traveling, but conservative and appropriate for this setting. Next, I whip out my Tarot deck—another no-no in the meditation center, but I'm desperate and the course hasn't officially started yet—to ask the cards for guidance.

The insight of my mini-reading is: "Yes, it's going be a hell of a lot of work for the next ten days. You'll feel burdened and at times overwhelmed, but there is a way out of misery. And the way out is to Be Yourself, meaning: even though you're in somewhat of a convent, in an incredibly structured, monastic setting, *Be Yourself.* Be enthusiastic, gregarious, adventurous, good-humored, and outspoken."

Well, that's gonna be interesting, I muse. *How to be outspoken, enthusiastic, and adventurous in a* silent *meditation retreat?*

But, the Tarot reading does put me into a better frame of mind. Freshly showered, with a tiny iota of confidence that I can make it through the next ten days, I bound down to the main office to greet my co-servers. All five of the women are serious, long-time Vipassana students—committed meditators who seem to have no problem following rules or sitting for long hours at a time. Immediately, I'm back to feeling like an imposter.

Our leader, a middle-class Indian woman called Bhavana, assigns our duties. I'm praying I do NOT get assigned something that is scarily vital. I'm hoping it's a menial job, so that if I screw up, there won't be any disastrous repercussions. Bhavana hands me my task list: I'm assigned as Chief Bell Ringer and Compounder. Five times a day, I'm responsible for getting the women—all 222 of them!—out of their catatonic slumber, into their saris, bindis and bangles, and moved into the main meditation Dhamma Hall—silent all the while. Yes, silently with no words, only bells, so they will be perched on their meditation cushions and ready to observe the workings of the mind with full awareness. And all before the teachers enter the hall.

Starting at four in the morning.

Uh-huh. This is India, people. A group of Indian women is not quiet, by nature. They like to chitchat, and they like to sleep. They don't deal with discipline, structure, and silence like European or American meditation students. From Day One, getting them off to the Dhamma Hall is one big cosmic joke.

At four a.m., after the main meditation gong goes *bing-bang-bong* around twenty times, it's my duty to go throughout my assigned block of five dorms and get these women moving. They look at me as if I'm IN-SANE. You've got to be kidding, their faces say. They're supposed to be observing Noble Silence for the entire ten days, which means no speaking, no miming, no eye contact. Yet, no matter what time of day, whenever I'm trying to get them on their merry way, they're either snoring, ignoring my bells, or caught twittering away amongst themselves. Or doing laundry, or showering and primping and chatting—when they're supposed to be perched on their cushions in the hall, in silence.

I feel more like Chief Cat Herder than Chief Bell Ringer. All of my control issues are in my face. How can I remain calm, compassionate, and equanimous when—as they walk past me with bangles tinkling, smirking and playing eye-contact games with their friends to sneak a conversation in away from my watchful, schoolmarm gaze—this is what's really going through my mind: *GET A MOVE ON, YOU LAZY ASSES!*

How far from calm, compassionate, and equanimous can THAT be?

It comes and it goes, the balance of my mind, the "sympathetic joy" I'm supposed to be cultivating as I attempt to *help* these women get through what is probably the most difficult ten days of their life. I wish someone who speaks Hindi would sit them down and explain to them that the silence is for their BENEFIT, that it will help them go deeper if they don't try to speak with their sisters, aunties, and grannies.

One dorm in particular, "J Block," where the brand-new students reside, is particularly problematic. J Block houses all green students, all very giddy, in a vast hall with no doors and only curtains to separate the beds—making for a stewpot of chitchat. Afternoons, I ring the little silver bell less than six inches from the ear of a woman pretending to be passed out asleep. She has complete cognition that I am endeavoring to get her attention, and she is ignoring me entirely.

But these women, I try to remind myself, are doing the best they can. In their daily life, it's un-HEARD of to remain silent with their female cohorts for an hour, let alone a whole day, or ten! I try to keep this in mind as somehow the lot of us makes it through the grueling days of Cat and Mouse. On Day Ten, the women are able to break silence—officially, that is, since they've been verbose all along. And, they reveal themselves as some of my greatest teachers, having embodied the Buddhist tale of Mara's Daughters.

See, when Siddhartha Gautama, the future Buddha, was meditating under the Bodhi Tree around 500 B.C., determined to reach enlightenment and vowing not to move from his seated posture until he was fully and completely awake, he had a stealthy visitor, the demon Mara. Diabolical Mara sent his ten daughters of distraction to tempt Gautama away from his journey of awakening. During that long, full moon night of the month of May, Mara's devilish daughters did their *darndest* to distract the future Buddha from his enlightenment endeavor.

It dawns on me that *my ladies of the "J Dorm" are Mara's Daughters, come to life in the Twenty-First Century!* They use every trick, every bit of sneaking and conniving possible to avoid my prodding, my bells, my hand-wringing pleas to get them to the meditation hall. They sneer and giggle behind my back. Some play opossum, and some flat-out ignore my existence.

On Day Ten, I keep in mind that "you catch more flies with honey than vinegar" as I make my way to J Block for the afternoon roundup. The period of Noble Silence has come to an end, but they still have to get to the meditation hall. But now, I'm on to them! I've come to realize that the only way to gain rapport with Mara's Daughters is to make a joke out of the whole thing, to laugh at the whole absurd set-up.

I approach J Dorm where ten of the worst troublemakers are piled onto one bed, hidden behind a curtain, SINGING Bollywood Hindi songs at the top of their lungs, expressing sheer glee at being set free from silence. Even though silence is technically over, students are requested to not sing or dance during the course, as it's still a "monastic" environment for the time being. Technically, I'm supposed to stop them at once.

But frankly, I'm tired of being Female Police Officer. I fling back the curtains to expose the nest of naughty ne'er-do-wells. They look at me expectantly, waiting for me to ring my little silver bell and reprimand them vigorously. Instead, I turn the tables. They have no idea that I possess lung power as loud as theirs, if not louder. I start belting out the first song that comes to mind, sure to be recognized in any language:

"HAPPY BIRTHDAY TO YOU! HAPPY BIRTHDAY TO YOU!!!!" I sing at the top of my lungs. The wily women are shocked. The Police Cop is Singing! The Police Cop is Singing! All of us then collapse into a collective fit of laughter. They realize I've been on their side all along. They know now, with the gift of coming through one of the most difficult, yet rewarding experiences of their lives, that my reprimanding was all for the best. Tough love, if you will.

I've still got a job to do. Somehow, I've got to get these women off to the meditation hall. And, now that silence is broken, there's no way they're going to break their gossiping to get moving. Since they don't speak a stick of English, there's no use explaining anything anyway, so, to get these ladies on their merry way, I call on my two best friends—Humor and Enthusiasm.

I figure, this is an agricultural land. If nothing else, they'll understand cow herding! I begin to make cow herding noses, clicking my tongue and yelling "Haaa! Haaa! HAAAH!" just as I've witnessed women doing in the fields of rural India. Then, I start mooing—"Moooooooooooooooo! MOOOOOOOOOO!"—and sweeping their ankles with a broom of rushes to get them moo-ving.

The Daughters of Mara let loose a hearty round of hysterical smiles, snickers, and snorts. They've got it! They've been acting like animals all along. Therefore, the Police Cop is going to treat them like animals!

They are still dragging ass, glimpsing in mirrors and taking their time. I reassure them that their bindis, bangles, and hair buns are all in place. *You look fabulous, darling. Get thee to the meditation hall, sister.* More shooing, mooing, and rush-brooming. And, miraculously, move on, they do! Some of them actually seem happy to oblige as we mutually, merrily MOOve toward the main hall.

The Daughters of Mara reveal the power of levity and lightheartedness the next morning, the last morning of the course. As usual, I enter their dorm at 4 a.m.—when I couldn't before stir the dead—to find ALL the J Dorm Daughters wide-awake, dutifully dressed, sitting on the edge of their beds, ready to go and waiting for me.

I am shocked, and happy! I enter the dorm and cheerily call out, "Good Morning, Ladies!" to which they respond, "Good morning!" and off they scurry to the hall behind me, just like a chattering charge of chicks following a mother hen. I don't even have to ring the bell once. And I don't have to moo, either.

What was that word again? En-LIGHT-enment? Oh yes! Keep it *light*. It's all gonna be alright.

Bhavatu Savva Mangalam
May All Beings Be Happy

And now, a Buddhist interlude to accompany our meditation missive—from *The Paddhana Sutta,* or "The Great Struggle": The Nirvanic nature of impermanence is very potent, so the demon Mara fights against it to keep us from realizing the Truth. These are the ten daughters (also known as soldiers) of Mara, the destroyers of meditation:

1. Desire to enjoy sense pleasures.
2. Unwillingness to reside or be happy in a quiet place, due to not wanting to be quiet because of the turmoil within.
3. Hunger—unsatisfied with food or alms given.
4. Craving for specific tastes and food.
5. Drowsiness, sloth, torpor.
6. Not wishing to be alone—fear of solitude.
7. Doubt (about whether one can be successful in meditation).
8. Becoming proud and arrogant when the meditation is successful.
9. Becoming well-known, receiving many offerings, gaining much respect and homage (concerning the teacher).
10. Following a false Dharma, creating a new and special Dharma in order to acquire abundant offerings, praising oneself and looking down on others.

Yes, all temptations most definitely exhibited by my Daughters of Mara, as well as myself, on this most recent voyage of self-discovery. How true, we are all mirrors for each other—let us give thanks for our button-pushers for they show us our most potent triggers!

Just Beachy

6th of December, Konkan Coast

I've just landed at the beaches of southwest India—a hectic haul from the gilded gates of the Vipassana meditation center. My mega-travel day began predawn three days ago. The prearranged rickshaw was NOT waiting for me at the gates as planned—really, no surprise there. I ended up schlepping my rucksack in the dark for three kilometers as fast as my still-sleeping legs could carry me to the railway station. I had to practically sprint with a full load on my back to make the train. If nothing else, India teaches flexibility and the ability to think QUICKLY on your feet.

Thus followed a very sooty overnight train journey—lots of tunnels means lots of grime through open Sleeper Class windows—followed by a dead-to-the-world sleep in a retiring room at a remote railway station, followed by two bumpety-bump-bump buses, followed by a long dusty traverse by foot over hill and dale, to finally collapse on the beach—a little slice of paradise on the Indian Ocean.

Sigh... it's so good to be here. I'm taking a week at the beach before I head further south to a yoga ashram for Christmas. Nothing planned beyond the paradisiacal perfection of pineapple and sunshine. And sleeping in—way past four a.m.

Darkala

20ᵗʰ of December, Varkala

It's a pitch-black evening. You walk back to your bungalow, located behind a wide stretch of restaurants and music bars. An Indian man stealthily reaches out to grab your breast as he passes by. Expletives that would make a sailor blush spew from your lips in response.

You wake up in the middle of the night, thirsty. You make to grab a glass of water on the bedside table. Luckily, you switch the light on first. You reach over to see The World's Largest Cockroach crawling out of your glass.

Greeting the new day, sipping coffee and journaling on your terrace as the sun rises, you glance over to see a pair of ravens five feet away, ripping out the entrails of a rat. Two mangy dogs then get into a scrappy fight, stealing the rodent remains from the birds as your stomach turns. You watch the scene in grotesque fascination.

With a half-second warning, the overhanging palm tree directly in front of your bungalow gives a rustle, and a weighty coconut falls— *splat*—to the ground, bursting open its white fleshy guts upon landing. *Lovely,* you muse. *Falling coconuts—a main cause of tourist deaths in South Asia.*

Welcome to My World of late. For the past week, I've been marooned in the Tourist Trap beach town of Varkala, in the southwest state of Kerala. Many travelers adore Varkala. I, on the other hand, have nicknamed this place, "Darkala."

I'm stuck here until I can get a train north back up to Karnataka—it being Christmas high season, everything is booked. I had traveled down to Kerala to take a "yoga vacation" at an ashram outside the capital city of Trivandrum (now renamed the unpronounceable Thiruvananthapuram—get your mouth around that one), but I left the place after twenty-four hours. The overbearing ashram program felt like nails on a chalkboard and I was judging everyone and everything in sight—a horrid attitude all around, and one I chose not to project on the poor, well-meaning people who were actually serious about the whole thing. So, I swiftly transformed into "The Flying Nun," fled through the ashram gates and hightailed it out of there to regroup at the nearest travelers' hub I could get to. Hence I am now here, in "Darkala."

It's been a rough week. I hit an attitudinal wall and lost my sense of humor, overcome by the heat, lack of proper nutrition, and incessant harassment by pesky vendors. The last thing you want to do in India is lose your sense of humor. But, my Happy Juices seemed to have run out somewhere along the coastline. Gee, I wonder if it has anything to do with some of the following hassles and hooey:

1. The Latest Scam

I don't recall ever having been warned about this ploy. A manager creates a potentially confusing situation between two customers (for example, a couple) in a shop or café that they frequent regularly together. They will tell each person, individually, that the other person did not pay before leaving the shop or café. It's been a few days—you can't remember and the other person can't remember—so you feel obliged to just pay again. After all, it's just a few dollars, right? But after this occurs a few times you start thinking, "*Hmmm*."

2. The Two-Week Holiday Hoopla

Varkala heavily attracts merrymakers from Europe who are here for two to three weeks for their winter holiday. This creates a vastly different vibe than the one found in long-term budget backpacker haunts. Prices are jacked up sky-high; after all, the Pound Sterling is incredibly strong, anyway, right? Costs of food, guest houses, and sundries are double. Alcohol, flowing freely, puts another spin on the interaction with the locals. Drunk Indian men, overly friendly on the dance floor, add a special twist.

3. Vampiric Vendors

With such a small window of sales opportunity between monsoon and hot seasons, the short tourist season means that all shopkeepers have their eye on hawking and harassing you to BUY, BUY, BUY. You can't walk ten feet from your door to get a cup of chai without navigating past a dozen hustlers. It's like they're putting octopus tentacles out to nab you every time, and it takes an incredible effort to stay non-reactive. The incessant chorus: *"Hello, Friend! How are you!? Come into my shop! Eat nice fish at my restaurant. You're a star! Come look! Hello! Hello! Oooh, you are model!"*

Now add begging dogs, wailing mosques, crying children, sneaky swamis, and more to the mix. I sometimes feel like I'm going to clock someone.

Ah, yes, this is the great equalizer of India travel—the shadow side that separates Those Who Lose Their Patience from Those Who Are Willing to Deal.

Musical Healing

22nd of December, Varkala

The worst of my morbid mood is finally receding. My aura must have gone through the drive-through psychic car wash with the fresh energy of a New Moon and Winter Solstice afoot, heralding the Coming of the Light.

Not only that, it never hurts to ask for help when you're feeling particularly out of sorts. Walking along a Varkala beach path yesterday, committing to a change of attitude, I came across a small, makeshift, rudimentary temple. With sweet, shambled statues of Vishnu, Shiva, Krishna, and Saraswati inviting me to pay my respects, I knelt down in the sand. *Help,* I prayed meekly. *That's about all I can muster right now. You know what I need. I'm overheated, malnourished, grumpy as all hell, and exhausted. Help.*

Oh, and—of course—thanks, guys. I dropped two rupees in the plastic offering cup, thanked the young caretaker who was draping a fresh garland of flowers around the neck of Vishnu the Preserver, and dragged-ass back to my guest house to take a sweltering nap. (The power is cut off in the middle of the day here—during the time when the ceiling fan would be your only hope. You've no choice but to sweat it out.)

Post-siesta, I mustered the strength to face the heat, get back out there, and (sound the trumpets!) BUY A GUITAR! This...THIS is the reason I had to come to dreadful Darkala! For two months, I've been looking all over India for a guitar. The other day, I asked a lovely woman from the U.K., called Faye, if she knew where I might get one in this tourist town. "Oh, yes, lovey," she replied in her incredibly charming Cockney accent. "Dere's woman called Angel who owns a beau'y parlor over on da cliff. Her partner, Matthias, is from Germany, an' 'e buys an' sells very nice guitars fer travelers."

Perfect! And today was the day! I skipped over to said location just as soon as my overheated self could motivate. Sure enough, there was the beautiful Indian Angel, smiling away, her half-Keralan, half-German baby son, Aaron (who, it turns out, is named after Elvis' middle name), gurgling in her arms.

Next, I met her husband Matthias, originally from the Black Forest. He showed me two steel-string acoustics. One was a big boy, Johnny Cash-style. The other, I knew immediately, was my New Best Friend. She's a sweet, medium-sized beauty—perfect for starters—and even comes with a plug-in for amplification, though I'm sure we'll give it a month or two before we start rockin' the rafters.

Now, my fingertips are raw and raging as I am working on my first batch of songs with chords downloaded from the Internet. I'm trying to practice at least two hours a day, learning a few songs at a time. I'm looking forward to holing up somewhere and plucking out the New Year perched on my straw mat at sunset.

Yesterday afternoon—sitting on my bed with the door open, the friendly old man who owns my bungalows came snooping around as I was practicing the guitar. The old man's name is *Murli Manohar*—a name for Krishna in the form of The Flute-Playing God.

I had just started picking out Dylan's "One More Cup of Coffee"—an eerily soulful and bittersweet ballad—when the toothless, loin-clothed Murli Manohar established himself on my stoop and indulged in a private concert. His English is practically nil, so I could tell his response by the whoops and hollers of praise.

After I finished the song, he blurted something out excitedly in the local language of Malayalam, smiled widely, wagged his dirty finger in the air, and disappeared. Moments later, he returned with something in his hand, paused, and respectfully wobbled his head in a manner that inquired whether he had permission to enter my room.

"Yes, yes, OK, *ji*," I replied.

He bounded over to my makeshift traveling altar, which has photos of my mother and father, pictures of Shakti and Shiva, Maa Kali, some dried flowers from the beach kids, a rose quartz, and a miniature, sealed *kumbh*—a tiny pot of water from the holy Ganges.

"Here!" he joyously declared, placing his offering on my altar. "For you! Music! Krishna! Krishna!" I set my guitar down and came over to see what he'd gifted me with: it was a little cardboard cutout drawing of Lord Krishna, the Flute Playing God of Music.

"Oh! Thank you, *ji*." I bowed my head to Krishna's namesake—hands in respectful, *namaste* prayer position, deep in gratitude. Murli then leaped out my front door with glee, gushing incomprehensible Malayalam words of musical encouragement.

Music, magic, *darshan* of gods, joy and laughter—I can feel them returning to my spirit with the Solstice and the Coming of the Light. Indeed, precious moments like these give me strength to endure the shadowy side of India—until the good times roll again.

Down the Rabbit Hole

6ᵗʰ of January, Konkan Coast

As impressions and experiences of India sweep over me with gale force, often it feels as if the lobotomy procedure—the one that began during my first journey here—is cutting much, much deeper.

Upon returning to the U.S. from India, I had such a hard time re-adjusting to modern American society, all I wanted was to return to the subcontinent to complete the lobotomy process, the rewiring of my brain. I needed an irreversible infusion of the priceless gifts of awareness, spiritual expansion, and creative awakening. I wanted to go full bore down the magical rabbit hole, so that when I ultimately resettled in the West, I'd have a completely new framework of perception—one that would not be so easily shaken or forgotten.

"Be careful what you ask for, you just might get it," I'm reminded. It took me almost four years to return. Now that I'm here, and I've dropped down that rabbit hole, I absolutely feel like *Alice in Wonderland.*

As my mom likes to playfully chide me, "You ask for it, you got it, Toyota." Lobotomy, indeed. My dark days in Varkala marked an end of the innocence of my India journey. Spiritually beat up, a little scarred and worse for the wear, I humbly hightailed it back to my chosen beach home—a sheltered coastland along the Arabian Sea on the Konkan Coast.

On Christmas Day, I miraculously got a train north from Darkala.

I've returned to my little stretch of heaven, hanging in my hammock amongst the coconut and betel nut groves. This is my respite—and here I'll remain, happily sipping papaya juice until I turn orange, or some equally enticing twist bounds its way into my play. My soul is much more joyful in this neck of the jungle.

There are no direct roads to this beach—one must schlep their stuff two kilometers over the hill, or hire a boat—so the traveler that finds his or her way here has a little something special within. Call it grit, call it a desperate need for peace and serenity. Call it what you will. I call it a specialized homing beacon for paradise and magical lands.

And magic it is. I'm awed on a daily basis by the enchantment in the air. Imps and faeries, goblins and trolls, pixies and pilgrims—the whole cast of characters from your favorite childhood fairy tales are right here on this beach.

It's never entirely free and easy in the land of magic. At times, true to form of any good Grimm story, Hans Christian Andersen adventure or Lewis Carroll concoction, a fairy tale can be frightening. One never knows what's around the next bend. Danger is afoot. There are vipers on the paths, rats in the roofs, and stingrays in the surf.

Some nights, I lie in my hammock strung between two coconut trees outside my hut, snuggling into my sleeping bag like a banana in its peel, ready for launch into my other life—the Dreamtime. To my east, just beyond the jungle, the Moon rises over the Western Ghats mountain range. As *Chandra* the lunar goddess emanates Her rays over my drowsy body, I hear rustling in the towering trees above my head. I try to make out the sound: Is it a crow, aiming to shit on me? A coconut about to conk on my head? Or simply the evening breezes whispering secret, sweet nothings? *Ah well*, I eventually conclude. *One must sleep, and one must trust.*

Besides, sleeping *inside* isn't easy. My hut houses a family of mice that sometimes force me to leave with their *squeak, squeak, squeak*-ing. No longer do I attempt to keep fruit in my hut overnight. I also have several resident indoor spiders—dream weavers in Native American tradition have become a number-one totem. My first week in the hut, I'd dream of spiders, then awaken, and turn on my head lamp to come face to face with a huge furry, fangy arachnid—the size of a spread-out hand, pulsing with life and raw presence—standing guard on my water bottle or sprawled out on my rucksack. Intermittently through the night, I'd wake up to see spiders in each corner of the hut. I'd say a little prayer to the Spirit of the Spiderwomen: "OK, we can share this hut, m'ladies, just please don't crawl on my face, or bite me."

Once the crows quiet down, the rats stop rustling, the spiders find their web, and the ants have bit their way across my mattress enough times (we don't even need to mention mosquitoes, now, do we?), and I'm lulled by the lapping waves of the mighty ocean, I let the whispering breezes from the jungle soothe me to slumber and dreamland.

But the real dreaming seems to occur in waking life, as this beach attracts a community of oddballs, misfits and mystics. The whole cast of the comedy of errors hides out in this magical rabbit hole for the entire season. We're a makeshift family of divine fools.

Occasionally, a group of "passers-by," fall down the hole—backpackers *en route* stopping by for a day or three, or even a week. But they quickly realize they're not going to get many creature comforts here—creatures, yes; accommodation comforts, no. They have to come to terms with the mud floor or straw door, or find their way back to upscale Goan beaches, where things like beds and mattresses, electricity, toilets, and showers are ready at the helm.

It is the long-term, seasonal residents that bring the beach to life, making for a real-time animation feature that would give the likes of Disney, Spielberg, and Lucas a real run for their wizardry money. Just to give you a taste—here's a few *freaks fabuleaux* that would make their way into the script.

1. The Divine Madman

A Russian schizophrenic, Ivan. One never knows if he is "on" or "off."

Playing with a full deck or short a few marbles? It's easy enough to write Ivan off as a lost soul; but then, as a Divine Madman is wont to do, he'll suddenly toss out a gem of a phrase, a missing link, in the midst of a slew of verbal dribble. He might invoke in you the spirit of Saraswati, the goddess of music and writing—just at the moment you were doubting that you could ever learn guitar—by randomly shouting her name out to you across the café.

Ivan only occasionally wears his false teeth, giving him a precious, happy-go-ghoulish appearance. He evokes compassion in me when I see him wandering the beach in the morning, dazed look on his face, muttering about building a royal family and a Russian kingdom, and something about Anna Karenina.

2. The Seeker of the Sacred

B.J., from L.A., is a long-term resident of the subcontinent—he's been here upwards of six years, with no return to the West in sight. B.J. is a spiritual renunciate, or modern-day baba. Traveling with only a few possessions and even fewer rupees, he's taken a hard path—one of immersing himself into the sacred rites and rituals of Indian sadhus. B.J. tells me he is viewed with skepticism and is even disdained by his native Indian counterparts, who aren't sure what to make of this American baba practicing their traditional path. As a result, B.J. is convinced that a number of gurus and babas are practicing black magic on him.

Once, after receiving an unsolicited blessing mark (a *teeka* of paint marking the third eye) by an Indian sadhu on the beach, he proclaimed to me that the man had cursed him. That night, B.J. had intense nightmares and visions, and his head began to pound. The tree outside his hut began to smell like human feces. In the morning, I tried to reassure him he could walk away from such negative energies, and dispel it as the illusion it surely is. But he would have none of it, and the next time I saw B.J., he was hightailing out of his hut, meager possessions in tow, off to find a nest where the energy was not so dark.

Are his fears real? What *is* real, anyhow? When I think back to my time in "Darkala," where I hit a spiritual rock bottom a few weeks ago, I'm reminded that one is bound to come across the occasional troll or hobgoblin in Wonderland from time to time. Whether the tape playing is live or Memorex—it doesn't really matter if it's splitting your head in two, now, does it?

3. The Faeries of the Flowers

I have come to adore the precious little girls who sell strands of flowers every evening on the beach. They'll approach me in their singsong voices while I am meditating, doing yoga, or practicing guitar: "Sapna... flower?"

I am especially fond of the very youthful 15-year old, Kavita, the daughter of the owner of my jungle huts. Kavita comes by the hut daily and listens to me pluck my guitar as I attempt to croon some folk-rock number and my fingers struggle to find that elusive F-chord. Mornings, Kavita sells fruit to the tourists on the beach, carrying a heaving basket of produce atop her jet-black, braided tresses. I buy pineapples, coconuts, bananas, and papaya from her regularly. Even when I hem and haw, saying no thank you, I don't need anything today, she starts cutting up the pineapple and placing the yummy nuggets in a baggie for me to eat later. Smart girl. She knows I'm a sucker for nature's own sweets.

In the evening, Kavita sells tiny flower leis, which I dutifully purchase with glee—only 12 cents a strand. Happily, she has begun to get a wee bit more comfortable in my presence—she has probably figured out that I'm not going anywhere anytime soon—and gives my hand a quick squeeze upon saying goodbye. We had a nice girly moment the other day as I pulled out a little bottle of nail polish—Kavita and her older sister painted their toes a lovely deep burgundy before hustling off to sell their fruity wares to the sunbathers.

Kavita calls me "Sapna," as do her friends, the other Flower Faeries. I see their smiling brown faces at sunset, their colorful skirts whipped by the wind and their strands of posies dangling from their wrists, and my heart simply melts with joy for the innocent beauty found in the spirits of children.

4. The Queen of Wands

And who might this mystical character be? I think you already know her quite well. Her intuitive skills are in great demand. Once the news hit the etheric airwaves that astrological consultations and tarot readings were available on the beach, Sapna was inundated with opportunities to be of service. It seems she should have a sign on her mud hut: "Come on by and get yer cards read, yer aura cleansed, yer horoscope analyzed! Head-sorting done here!"

Yes, get your head sorted, because even if you're Alice herself wandering through Wonderland, occasionally you need a check in—a landing pad. A cozy stoop you can sit on for an hour or three and recalibrate. When India is fiddling with the cerebral dials, performing psychic surgery, Goddess knows a proper spiritual midwife is in order.

I don't know if I am, in fact, that midwife. Yet, I do try to assist the traveler in birthing whatever transformational, mind-blowing baby that's just begging to be born. On that note, it's time to put on my paranormal parachute, don my divine diving gear, and join my fearless flock of freewheelin' faeries and electric elves for sunset. A girl ought to be properly prepared if she is going to plunge headlong down the rabbit hole of creative rebirth and transformation, right?

The Queen of Wands

9th of January, Konkan Coast

Two weeks ago, a wandering, saffron-robe wearing French baba approached me out of the blue and gave me a long bamboo staff—a real wand. He said I would need it—it would be useful to keep away pesky cows and bad businessmen.

I was so honored! Indeed, I needed a magic wand to protect me. Sadly, out of complete carelessness, I left the wand somewhere in the nearby jungle that very same day! For days after, every time I saw the French baba, I would have my tail between my legs, ashamed at my carelessness with the enchanted gift.

But, lucky, lucky me—the stars are on my side! Yesterday late afternoon, I came across my Flower Faeries on the beach. I bought a super-sized, special strand of vibrant orange marigolds, intending to bring these powerful Shiva blossoms home for protection and blessing. At my hut, I draped the flowers on a large stick leaned against my little door, to honor the staff that had disappeared over ten days ago. "I'm sorry I lost you," I told the substitute wand. "I promise to look after my things better next time."

Five minutes afterward, it was sunset, so I headed out to the beach where I bumped right into the French baba. We chatted a bit—Ça va? Ça va!—when a spark of recognition came into his twinkling blue eyes.

"Your staff! I am knowing where is it!" Baba says with a gentle French accent. "You DO?!" I respond. Before Baba can nod his head, he darts off into the jungle and disappears for about fifteen minutes. I wait and watch Surya the Sun make his way to the horizon, when Baba returns with my magic wand in tow.

Sure enough, it was the same sturdy staff—we recognized the markings at the bamboo base. I had carelessly left it leaning against a tree or hut somewhere during my ramblings, and two weeks later, this wandering wizard recovered my trusty tool.

I felt honored and validated—I am definitely on the right track in Wonderland. Now, my magic wand stands tall in a corner of my hut, and sleeps beside me, so we can keep a keen eye on each other.

Remember, somewhere in another galaxy—far, far away—wizards, wands, faeries, and wandering priests are alive and thriving.

Beach Witch

26th of January, Konkan Coast

Roz, 24, from Canada, has been a mystical, spritely sister to me ever since I first arrived to the beach in December. With her dark hair and understated elegance, she is quick to laugh, revealing dimples and inner magic. We share so many characteristics—even a bit of the same Native American bloodline—that many locals refer to us as sisters.

Yes, Roz could be a younger version of myself. She is a brilliant source of light and intuition. It's been a gift to have a playmate to read Tarot with and ponder the planets, marveling daily over the special "genie in a bottle" quality of India. We have cracked ourselves up with the ability to dream up something we would like to manifest, and then—"BOING!"— just like the old TV show, *I Dream of Jeannie*, our wishes are granted. It's like Aladdin's lamp, with a twist: sometimes our "spells" backfire—just enough to make things a little cockeyed and more than a little interesting.

Take, for example, the time we created a New Moon medicine wheel at the top of a nearby cliff, overlooking the Arabian Sea at sunset. After saluting the four directions, lighting our candles, and making offerings of coconuts and flower wreaths to the Goddess, we meditated inside the circle to receive guidance and insight for the next lunar cycle.

Simultaneously, we noticed a theme of the color white surrounding us in nature. A white mother dog known to us from our beach followed us all the way, and graced us with her presence. A flurry of white bird feathers lay just outside the circle. Our flowers were white, as were our candles. We came to the conclusion that our shared message was one of purity—love's transparency—symbolized by the predominance of the color white.

At that instant, a "white out" came. Out of nowhere, we heard a slight humming. Suddenly, thousands upon thousands of tiny white moths swarmed around our head. It was completely out of control! They infiltrated our hair and our clothing, darted in and out of our faces. We looked around and outside the medicine wheel—the moths were nowhere else to be found, except within the four-foot space where we stood. Was our own white light emanating so bright, that all the moths were drawn to our flame? The onslaught was so fast and furious, we could not continue. Quickly, we blew out our candles, grabbed our bags and—half-laughing, half-panicked—we hightailed it off the hilltop as fast as we could. It reminded me of a children's book I adored as a little girl, *Half Magic*, where the spells are working but are slightly skewed—until the novice magicians get the hang of it.

Two days after The White Moth Incident, Roz wanted to experience a little beach romance. She boldly declared to the Universe, "If it's going to happen, it has to happen NOW, or I'm leaving this place!" Well, true to form, be careful what you ask for—you just might get it! Less than six hours later, Roz had herself a sweet paramour, a young Israeli man. He told her that he'd been eying her for some time, and that he saw great potential for their relationship, and perhaps she'd like to travel with him? It seems the spell was over the top. She wanted to have a suitor, but not a vigilante pursuer! Just like the flurry of white moths, the young knight in shining armor swarmed into Roz's life faster than you can say, "A-la Peanut Butter Sandwiches!" Within 24 hours, her Insta-Romeo had moved himself into an adjoining hut next door to her own, and began inundating her space and belongings with little white notes. All through the next few days, Roz found romantic snippets of prose in her hammock, her beach bag, her blankets. Every time she turned around, a little Romeo reminder fell out of her stuff—just like the white moths. "Turn it off! Turn it off!" We laughed together at the love spell gone awry.

Roz and I decided we needed to submit a pilot to *Saturday Night Live*, the WB, or even ABC. Think *Baywatch* combined with *Charmed*. Add a huge helping of farce, the likes of *SNL*. Take two warm-hearted, well-meaning beach bimbos, who happen to have a little magic in their DNA. Spells with the best of intentions are just a little lacking in the accuracy department, and you've got the basis for something wonderfully wacky, terrifically tacky, and superbly successful cooked up in the cauldron. Throw in a little *Charlie's Angels* and—voilà! You have *Beach Witch*!

Local Cola

30ᵗʰ of January, Konkan Coast

Sometimes two ships pass silently in the night. On some occasions, the ships sidle up next to each other, the sea captains share a tale or two and they hit it off to forge a new alliance. Perhaps, the intrepid mariners even decide to chart a new course altogether—in tandem. Indeed, in my own recent charting of the starry skies, it is this scenario that has come into play.

On Boxing Day, after those two horrible weeks in Darkala, I returned via bus and train back to my little beach retreat. At journey's end, too pooped to schlep my stuff the final two kilometers, I hired a fisherman to take me by boat for the last leg of the trip. When the little wooden ship was near enough to shore, I threw myself over the side, walked in waist-high water to the sand, then practically fell on my knees, with this solemn vow:

O Mother India, I promise that I shall not leave this sacred beach home until something grabs me firmly by my heartstrings and pulls me, unmistakably, away to distant shores. Think Scarlett's declaration at the finale of *Gone With the Wind*—"I shall never go hungry again!" Yes, a little Drama Queen-esque, but oh-so-true!

Now, five weeks later, it does indeed appear that something is pulling me—by my heartstrings—away from here. I'm being summoned, pulled, guided by a force greater than my own. Some call it love.

Feeling strong and fully recovered from December's darker days, I had a plan nailed down as of the New Year: Yes, that's it! I would hole up, secluded and solo, until Shivaratri—the most important Hindu religious festival in India, taking place on February 18 this year—and not move an inch from my beach.

And then one day, the archetypal mysterious stranger walks into my favorite café, altering completely the events of the day...

I've just settled down for a long, hot, India-winter's nap in The Oasis, a family-run chai shop that's just a skip and a hop from my hut. I'm reclining on the restaurant's straw mats atop a cool concrete slab, drinking a lemon soda and writing in my journal. After fifteen minutes or so, I get groggy and feel a sultry siesta coming on, and so I prepare to head back to my hammock for some serious napping.

But a little voice tells me to stay put, right where I am. It's one of those moments where an invisible hand pushes you back down in your seat. *That's odd. Okay, I'll stick around. It's not like I've got a big to-do list or anything.* So I surrender to stay in the café, lean back in my perch, and proceed with daydreaming, staring aimlessly at the palm-frond makeshift roof.

With one ear, I listen happily to the husband-and-wife proprietors, Parvati and Ganesh, chatting back and forth in their native language of Kannada. Their days consist of preparing endless rounds of banana pancakes, fruit salad with curd, and chai after chai after chai for the Westerners. Their feisty toddler son, Somu, is the real center of attention, as he darts back and forth between the kitchen and the tourists' tables, coaxing out games and playmates wherever he can. I'm the only Westerner there this lazy afternoon—everyone else is sleeping or sunning on the beach. Enjoying the twittering of the two-year-old, I realize how pleasantly peaceful and serenely satisfied I am to be a part of a family home, and begin to doze off in this cafe-*cum*-living room. And then I overhear five words of destiny:

"Do you have local cola?"

A tall, attractive, blue-eyed young man has just blown into the cafe, like a whirlwind. He's got a buzz about him, as if he hasn't fully settled into the dreamy cocoon that the long-term beach residents seem to be wrapped up in. He's moving quickly, talking swiftly, and, by my lightning-flash estimation, traveling quickly. The fact that he has asked the proprietors for a "local cola" instead of Coke or Pepsi means that he's not a typical tourist: he's a hardcore traveler, recently arrived from "real India" where Thums Up, Limca and Mazza are the soft drink standards.

What is "real India"? It's India-on-the-move. It's India-in-your-face. It's rickshaw wallahs, shysters and grinning vendors, and prolific pungent odors that make your stomach do somersaults. And, it's far removed from the gentle jewel of gestation, laziness, and easy-living that is this very south Indian beach.

Something in my gut tells me to strike up a conversation with this good-looking fellow. Perhaps it is my curiosity, since I've gotten comfortable over the past month: *How is it "out there" in the trenches?* Perhaps I want to chat with another practical, frugal-minded backpacker (local cola is about half the price of western brands).

But, let's be honest here, Bindi dear.

A tall, attractive, blue-eyed stranger on his own. Is there, perchance, another motivation at work?

Hmmm, let me think.

I rouse myself from my chaise repose, turn toward his nearby table, and break the proverbial ice.

"Did you just get to the beach?" I ask.

And he answers: Yes, indeed, he has. In fact, he has bicycled here.

All the way from Prague, Czech Republic.

That's over 12,000 kilometers, folks, on two manual-powered wheels. Through Russia, Kazakhstan, Kyrgyzstan, Afghanistan, the far reaches of the Himalayas in northern India, Rishikesh, Delhi, Rajasthan, Gujarat, Maharashtra. Down, down, down... all the way to south India, through

Goa, to this very spot.

Whoa. It takes a lot to impress me. But this guy may very well be one of the most bad-ass travelers I've yet to come across. And, I tell him just that—how impressed I am with his ambition, strength, and guts. And, I secretly think, his insanity. Anyone who rides his bicycle overland through Asia for upwards of one year is definitely crazy. In the very best way.

Just my type.

Fast forward two weeks later, Bindi is having a whole new kind of adventure. As a "we" instead of a "me"!

Jan (pronounce the 'J' as a 'Y'), 27, is a graphic designer and cartoonist from Prague—and just about as creatively cockeyed as yours truly. But we are as different as we are similar. It's "the mystic meets the pragmatist." Erin is a whole lotta San Francisco woo-woo and Jan is Central European "let's-do."

Surprisingly, with such an odd combo, Jan has become a magical mate of sorts. Jan had originally planned on staying on the beach for about three days, before cycling off to the holy village of Hampi, in the rocky, hot, high plains region of central India. But three weeks later, he's still here with me, and we have been up to all kinds of mischief. Amongst wide swaths of sunbathing, campfire cooking, boulder-hopping and beachcombing, we've had ample opportunity to fiddle with the guitar, contemplate the cards and stars, and mock up a new, revised travel itinerary.

Jan is ultimately hell-bent on heading to the Andamans, a remote group of islands off the coast of Myanmar (Burma) that belongs more culturally and ecologically to the tribes of Southeast Asia than the Indian subcontinent. It's a long journey to the Andamans—a week-long trip from here to the east coast port of Chennai (formerly Madras, and capital of the southeast state of Tamil Nadu) by road and rail, followed by a "slow-boat-to-China," three-day sea voyage across a massive stretch of the Bay of Bengal.

Jan's asked me to jump my solo ship, and climb aboard for a collaborative cruise. Having already met his goal of bicycling to the south of India, he's happy to carry his bike aboard bus and train for the ground stretch of the journey. In turn, I've ruminated, analyzed, and pondered this daring decision inside and out. I've examined my own star charts, contemplated my course, and come to a carefully considered conclusion: I've nothing to lose, and so much to gain. It's a golden key, a summons back to "real India," out of the proverbial womb of this beach cocoon, and a return to the fast track of rugged travel.

I've no idea what awaits. I *do* know that, without such a strong and steady copilot, I likely would not make it to such remote reaches and beaches on this particular trip. I also know that the only difference between lucky people and unlucky people is that lucky people say "yes" when opportunity knocks.

Thus, this Full Moon Friday, we depart on a pre-dawn *local* bus to the world heritage site of Hampi, a magical village strewn with majestic boulders and ancient, trippy temples. After Hampi, one chai at a time, Jan and I will make our way to the port of Chennai. If the shared seas are still smooth sailing, we'll hop aboard a big-old boat and make our three-day way to the Andamans, where a new potential paradise beckons.

This is, irrefutably, a huge gearshift for me. But change has always been my best friend. In fact, I get cranky, bored, and irritable when things start feeling a little too, shall we say, *normal*. Sometimes, life hands us a situation where we don't know the outcome, period. In such cases, we can stay stuck for days, weeks, or years. And sometimes, the only way out is through. *The Osho Zen Tarot* has a great description of diving in: "You can't work your way out by working it out with the mind. Better to follow your heart if you can find it. If you can't find it, just jump. Your heart will start beating so fast there will be no mistake about where it is!"

And so, off I jump! Prayers packed in my parachute, laughter lining my life jacket, leaping into the great unknown called the F-U-T-U-R-E. I've no doubt this tantalizing tangent will bring a bounty of experiences.

COWABUNGA!

Mirror, Mirror

February 14ᵗʰ, Chennai

"What happened on the way to Chennai? What happened to *the guy*?" read the emails from home. Enquiring minds wanted to know. Understandably: it's human nature to follow up on a fledgling love affair, especially given such exotic environs!

As I said before, if our romance had a name, it would likely be "The Mystic Meets the Pragmatist." Jan is the *Prague*-matist, in case you had any doubt. My last month spent traveling alongside the Czech has been about balance—balance between polar opposites: yin and yang, work and play, dark and light, wrong and right.

Certainly, contrast between two lovers is all well and good and makes for interesting plot lines, yes? But have I mentioned that Jan is an atheist, who sees life almost exclusively through the lens of the linear and rational? As my connection to Consciousness, in all its non-linear, wild and wooly forms, is the most important passion in my life, you can only imagine how confusing such a liaison can be. Sure, it's all fine and dandy in the context of casual friendship, but when you're delving into intimate waters, such a contrast in world views can make for some stormy sailing. I've not yet had such an intensive looking-glass before me 24-7, where I've been utterly *forced* to realize the deepest nature of my mind through amplified reflection.

I've learned that the intuitive, empathic, magical-reality mode in which I move in the world is not just some reasoned choice I've made; it's an inextricable part of my soul, of my entire being. And, it appears I'm powerless to change it, try as I might to contort my very nature to become less of a sixth-sense, soul-focused woman.

Still, I willfully decided to try it out, to plunge headlong into an alternative adventure with Jan.

Why? *Just to see what was there.* Like Alice, in Wonderland.

And, oh, how very much *is* there! To begin with, there is a lot of hard work. Traveling with Jan, I've learned that experiencing India primarily through the superficial mode of the five senses is a vastly different trip than I've been on. By "superficial" I don't mean lacking importance or depth; rather, I mean it in a WYSIWYG way—What You See Is What You Get.

JAN is all about getting his hands dirty in India through the physical: Scratch your shins while scaling the boulders; order fried brains off the Muslim restaurant menu just to try something new; walk through a Madras slum after nightfall *just to see what is there.*

ERIN is all about floating through India as if it were a dream designed exclusively for her: Plant your bum on a sandy dune at sunset; absorb the *prana* energy beamed down by Surya the Sun before he says *bon nuit;* lie in bed, writing, for hours before leaving the boudoir if the muse hits in the morning; sidle up to the sadhus and ponder the astral weather patterns *just to see what is there.*

A train-wreck of a romance waiting to happen? Perhaps, but don't forget that the word "disaster," from the Latin, means "unfavorable, from the stars." Stardust doesn't come without a price. Sometimes it takes a Big Bang—a serious clash of consciousness to create new frontiers.

It's as if two people stand on opposing banks of a river, the stream of collective consciousness. The individuals are shouting back and forth across the wide waters, the likes of the following:

Person A (Pragmatist)—"Hey, check it out! On this side of the river, there are loads of captivating flora and fauna, a well for drinking water, and a place where we can sleep under the stars *all night long!*"

Person B (Mystic)—"Hey, check it out! There's a medicine wheel mandala on this side! We can light candles and incense and sing 'Om Namah Shivaya' to the heavens *all night long!*"

Meanwhile, the static electricity muddies up the airwaves. You try again to make your side of the river sound even more enticing, using points of reference that make perfect sense—to *you*. When that doesn't quite work, you attempt to speak the other person's language and don their values, but it hurts, squeezes, pokes, and pinches like a pair of wrong shoes.

Exhausted from this clashing cross-current conversation, you throw your hands up in exasperation. Finally, one of you surrenders, calls it a day, and dives in to swim to the other's distant shore, foreign and alien to you as it is. Tuckered out, you welcome the other with open arms, and determine to enjoy yourself. Secretly, however, you wonder what your night might have been like would you have stayed on your side of the stream.

Sound pessimistic? Exhausting? Exhilarating?

Well, let's put it this way: if hard-core travel is about trying on new frameworks of reality, then Jan and I became the ultimate vagabonds by dealing with each other's frames of reference.

Of course, all work and no play make for very dull thrills for Jack and Jill. Even if your communication is a disaster, you can still have fun. Hard work pays off, and the truth is, I would not have experienced half of what I've enjoyed over the past five weeks were it not for Jan's practicality, curiosity, skill, motivation, and mode of travel. Ever since we started out on the road together, India has revealed herself to be more vast and beautiful than I could have ever imagined. For this, I have Jan to thank, and I have stories to share…

Rocky Mountain High

8th of February, Hampi

I was completely, utterly blown away by Hampi, housing the sacred stone ruins of the UNESCO World Heritage site of Vijayanagara in northeast Karnataka. Above and beyond the breathtaking temple complexes, never before have I beheld such intriguing and magnificent natural landscapes.

Our first day filled me with sheer exhilaration, scrambling to the top of Hampi's boulder-strewn hills just before sunset. Jan and I perched atop the highest boulder we could manage to scale and marveled at the sites before us: miles upon miles of beautiful rocky formations, lined with rice paddy fields, banana groves, Hanuman temples, and tiny villages tucked away amongst the boulder batches.

It was a high beyond heights, a panoramic splendor. As I soaked up the visible wavelets of energy surrounding my auric field at the top of the rock, India's map flashed through my mind. I contemplated the fact that the Indian subcontinent is considered by some to be the heart chakra of the Earth. If you glance at a map of India, you'll see that She is indeed shaped similarly to a heart. And the precious gem that is Hampi lies in the heart of the heart.

Our second night in Hampi's heart, we again ascended the boulder mountains. As the Full Moon climbed high in the sky above our heads, we lay under the stars and sang praises to Ganesha, the elephant-headed god. Even atheistic Jan's now hooked on a little Indian chanting, egging me on to sing "Ganesha Sharanam"—a real earworm of a mantra. Quite fine with me, as Ganesha is the Divine Remover of Obstacles, especially auspicious for travelers of both inner and outer realms.

Jan and I even ran into my soul sister, Roz, of *Beach Witch!* fame, who had arrived in Hampi the week before. The three of us played away the days, splashed around in a nearby reservoir, and bicycled through rice paddy fields and picturesque villages. We delighted with laughing children who hassled us for nothing more than the occasional "school pen" or "one cricket ball."

With such alluring natural beauty, Hampi pulled us in twice as long as we expected. But move on we had to, for it was Chennai or bust, where Jan's boat departing for the Andamans—presumably with me in it— would set sail in less than a week. So we strapped on our packs to make our way to Madras, the southeast port hub. Of course, due to my own distaste for preplanning, we made the decision to leave Hampi at the last minute for an overnight train journey. Without an advance reservation.

Midnight Express

9ᵗʰ of February, Hampi to Chennai

That evening, just before midnight, Jan and I boarded our train and nuzzled our way into the Second Class Non-AC Sleeper car, without reservations.

I was dead tired, recovering from a cold, and determined to use charm, or *baksheesh*, on the conductor to procure a bunk for the next ten hours. Jan, on the other hand, admitted he secretly wished we'd get booted to Third Class, for a little "harsh traveling fun." He wanted to test me a bit, to see if we could *endure* a shared night in general seating, sardine-packed Third Class.

Thanks, but no thanks. Not my cup of chai. I've done "hard India train travel" before, and I've had enough. Second Class Sleeper suits me just fine.

But the universe likes to respond to requests, verbalized or visualized. Jan got his wish. Neither charm nor money worked on the conductor. Our train was overbooked. We were ordered to leave the Sleeper car immediately. With no choice, at the next station, we ran to change cars before being booted off the train entirely. Schlepping our heavy packs, all of Jan's bicycle panniers and camping equipment, and my guitar, we barely squeezed our way into the Third Class car, just in time.

It wasn't the most harrowing general seating experience we could have had, and it could have been much worse. We didn't have to sleep vertical the entire night, standing in a cramped passageway between two train cars with forty other without-reservation passengers and their babies, ten sacks of rice, goats, and what-have-yous, as the door to the toilet goes *phwap-phwap*, open and closing next to you with the scent of urine wafting in your face all night long.

Lucky for us, we managed to get seats on a bench. We actually slept—albeit fitfully—in distorted postures. On our narrow perch, I tried to make myself comfortable, using Jan's contorted legs (he's over 6'3") as a makeshift headrest. A young Indian mother scooted next to me sometime in the middle of the night, taking advantage of six inches of available space. In no time, she made herself cozy on my own lap for the duration. The three of us slept on that bench like nesting Russian dolls. Eight men dozed on newspapers strewn on the floor beneath us. We all slumbered in some weird form of collective comfort as the train rumbled through 'til dawn, when we arrived in Bangalore to catch our connection for another eight-hour "express" to Chennai.

Kollywood

10ᵗʰ of February, Chennai

Arriving in Chennai, the southeast port-hub of the nation and capital city of Tamil Nadu state, it felt great to be thrust back into the pulse of urban "real India" once again. For four days, Jan and I encountered less than a dozen Westerners, Chennai being more of a transit hub and far down on the list of most travelers' itineraries.

What a relief for a change! Less tourists means less hassling. The most persistent heckling we encountered consisted of a barrage of callers asking, "Change money?" Hardly a hair-raiser. The worst rip-offs consisted of a few surprise "Price increases!" not listed on the restaurant menus, which cost us an additional five or ten rupees here and there. Manageable.

I still hadn't decided whether I'd accompany Jan to the Andamans. Two days before the ship departed from hot, sticky Chennai, we decided to treat ourselves with a little adventure involving air conditioning: a three-and-a-half hour blockbuster at the local cinema. Chennai has its own thriving Tamil-language film industry, it's own version of Bollywood, called "Kollywood."

What was the movie about? There were no subtitles, and it seemed more like bad MTV than HBO. I have no idea what it was about! But

I didn't care. I was just happy to be soaking up air-con and sipping flat Coke. Jan and I determined afterwards that the plot was something about an attractive young Tamil man, who owned a bookshop. Some bad people didn't like his success. So they hired some thugs to go in and bust the place up. Meanwhile, while driving across town, the discouraged bookseller meets a raven-haired beauty who fixes motorcycles in her free time. They like each other, then they argue, then meet again, then dance and sing in a meadow, just like a "Spring Wind" deodorant commercial. And, of course, it all works out in the end.

Cost of the Kollywood blockbuster? 95 cents.

Cost of a custom-popped, on-the-spot cone of masala spiced corn? 22 cents.

Value of soaking up air-conditioning for three and a half hours, not having to think one single thought because you couldn't understand anything onscreen if you tried?

Priceless.

Send In the Clowns

11ᵗʰ of February, Chennai

Jan and I had another opportunity to devour delicious *masala* pop-corn the very next evening, at the psychedelic version of The Greatest Show on Earth: The Great Royal Circus of Chennai, featuring (wink, wink) *authentic* Russian performance artists!

Now, this was bizarro big top at its finest. For $0.86 each, we witnessed the Russian version of the Addams Family take the stage with a terrific troupe of Tamil tightrope walkers, trapeze artists, and tantalizing trick-sters. Allow me to present my Favorite Freaks of the Circus:

Favorite Freak #1

The real talent pool of the bunch was found in one particular magic man—a real pro who, I'm convinced, must have been trained in ayurvedic *panchakarma*. Here was a specialist in the ancient art of purgation—the vomiting therapy known as *vamana*.

The bulky feathered-fez-sporting madcap strode confidently into the ring, gulping down gallons of green-tinted water from a bottom-less bucket, then rotated 360-degrees to face each member of the crowd, spewing out the very same green liquid like a human fire hydrant.

Favorite Freak #2

A streaked blonde Russian—think Morticia Addams meets a six-foot tall, well-built Jerry Hall. This circus siren has clearly embraced her life purpose with great gusto. Striding confidently around the ring in her stiletto cowboy boots—cracking her whip to great effect—the oddly hot, eerily strange razzle-dazzle Russian wiggled and jiggled, shimmied and shook her Moscow moneymaker with all she had, as every semi-erotic pose earned a few clucks and *tsk-tsks* from the conservative Indian crowd.

A few random whistles of praise spewed out of the 20-rupee "cheap seats" behind us, where the bidi smoke wafted to the rafters and the poorer families sat on bleachers with their extended families. Glancing behind us, Jan and I both agreed that next time—if there ever will be a next time to go to a circus in India—we'd opt for the cheap seats and join in the fun part of the house.

The Pause That Refreshes

13th of February, Chennai

Jan and I experienced many things as a duo that I may never have dared as a solo act. But, like an over-saturated sponge, I'd had enough intensity and sensory input for a fortnight of journaling fodder. I became so full I was overflowing. As a writer absorbing experience, I get pregnant with possibilities, and I need masses of space—and time—in solitude and silence, to collect my thoughts and insights. If I don't give attention where attention is due, the creative baby can't be born. And, as any artist, writer, performer can tell you, if one waits too long to make art, it's easy to get stagnant and stale. At best, we get wistful or moody.

At worst, we become the Queen of Cranky, which, unfortunately, is what I began morphing into, at the expense of our collective serenity. As bickering and bitching became the norm rather than the exception, my internal alarm signals began to sound—softly at first, then like an air-raid siren. In order to channel life's occasional overwhelm into healthier expressions, I'm reminded to keep the drama on the page—or stage, as the case may be. I've got to use the surges of transformational energy to create new stuff, rather than destroy the good stuff.

Fortunately, after many years of writing, I recognize the call to compose, the need for repose. When my external situation—and that includes relationships with others—becomes unbearably aggravating, it's a clue that I desperately need space and time to think, write, reflect.

In short, I need "the pause that refreshes."

After days of deliberation, it was clear I needed some major breathing room, and no matter how big that boat, if I joined Jan's journey to the Andaman Islands, I knew I'd turn into a stark raving lunatic. I already was close to banshee-bitch level. Thus, I made the difficult decision to delay my own departure for the Islands for a week or two. We said our goodbyes, with loose plans to meet anew across the ocean blue, and Jan bicycled off to the Port of Chennai for his own mega-marine voyage.

"It's high time to write, pray, and reconnect to spirit," I determined, quickly recalibrating my reality barometer back to its usual, sustainable levels—back to dreaming, guitar, writing, and the otherly realms of creative consciousness. It didn't take long to get reconnected. Within three hours of Jan's departure, I had a clear vision of my next destination—to celebrate the great night of Lord Shiva, at the holy hill of Arunachala.

Om Namah Shivaya

16th of February, Tiruvannamalai

Hello from Tiruvannamalai, in Tamil Nadu, southeast India. I've come here specifically for *Maha Shivaratri*, the great night of Shiva, universally revered as the most important religious festival for Hindus. Tonight, on the eve of the New Moon, it is said that Lord Shiva walks the Earth and offers liberation to all those who would worship Him.

Ah, sweet freedom! Thousands of pilgrims have come to pay homage to Shiva as an aspect of *agni*, or fire, in which he is known as Arunachaleswar. Tonight, at the peak of Mahashivaratri, I will join the masses as we circumnavigate the 14-kilometer base of the red-colored, holy hill Mount Arunachala, all the while softly chanting the mantra, "Om Namah Shivaya."

The mountain peak itself represents the male part of Shiva consciousness, the *lingam*, whereas the circular base represents the female aspect of Shakti—also called Kali or Parvati—as the divine round *yoni*.

It is said that Shiva appeared on this sacred mountain as a towering inferno—a beacon of light—in order to assist all of humanity, as well as his holy brothers in the triple godhead, Brahma and Vishnu, in releasing the ego from the chains that bind one in misery.

Certainly, gaining liberation from misery and suffering is enticing any day of the week, let alone lifetime. And, I've come here for more personal reasons. I have work to do.

It's time to make peace with Shiva.

During my first trip to India, I was deeply humbled through my experiences in Varanasi, another home to Shiva in the form of the destroyer: Varanasi is the place to honor the dead. Up until that point, I had an irreverent, cocky attitude toward the gods and goddesses of the Hindu pantheon. As a result, I learned the hard way—my time in Varanasi felt like a trial by fire.

Through the difficulties experienced at that Holi festival four years ago, I came to realize that these deities are alive, awake, and totally accessible for devout Hindus; their existence isn't even a question. And, *especially* while I am a guest in this land, to ignore or, worse, to mock their importance is a monumental no-no, to say the least.

Fast-forward to here and now: I've arrived here in Tiruvannamalai, in the middle of dry, dusty nowhere, to clear my mind, fuel my spirit, and open my heart—and most importantly, in some small way, to make up with Shiva. To ask for his pardon for the smug way I behaved in his stomping grounds up north.

It's working—this new, humble approach. Straight off the four-hour, oddly smooth bus ride from Chennai, I found a fantastic little hotel room just off the main temple bazaar. Clean, quaint, attached bath (we won't talk about the cardboard bed) for US $1.50/night. Yes, every now and again the guidebook comes through, and you find a guest house that actually matches the price and description as described!

Following a most excellent night's rest, I enjoyed a tasty breakfast of *idly*—lentil flour dumplings—dipped in coconut chutney and spicy *sambar* sauce. I then gathered my belongings into a day bag, covered up my bare shoulders, put on a long skirt, and headed into the baking hot sun toward the massive ten-hectare Arunachaleswar Temple complex.

After circumnavigating the main shrine, a massive Shiva lingam, I spotted a small enclosure just off the main throughway. Tucked away in this somewhat-hidden altar cove was a delightful statue of Shiva in his form as Lord of the Dance, Nataraja. The deity Himself was draped in garlands upon garlands of orange, yellow, red, and white flowers. A lone, white-haired old man in a clean, white *lungi* sat in full-lotus position, meditating unobtrusively, off to one side of the side of the altar and facing the deity. Silently, I perched behind him, humbly sharing a meditation moment.

It is said that Shiva is not just an aspect of divine consciousness, but rather, Shiva IS divine consciousness. I wonder if this is why, for the first time in weeks, when I closed my eyes before this dancing deity, I felt peace and serenity wash over me like a cool breeze. Feeling refreshed after a few minutes, I opened my eyes to take in my surroundings. At that moment, an elderly female sadhu quickly strode out of an adjoining enclave. I noticed dozens of colorful flowers strung through gray dreadlocks piled atop her head.

"OM Namah Shivaya! OM Namah Shivaya!" she declared, as she raised both hands high to the sky, then fully prostrated herself in surrender and piety—arms stretched forward, legs straight out behind her, facedown—before the deity. I was touched, and inspired by the sight of this majestic woman of God, shamelessly offering herself before her Lord.

A few minutes later, the old man in the white lungi roused himself from meditation. Matching the abilities of the best yoga teachers in San Francisco, he lowered himself in a perfect *chaturanga dandasana* yogic plank position to the floor, offering his own prostrations before the deity.

Wow, I thought. *I would do well to do the same, right here, right now, and follow his lead. After all, what am I here for, but to make peace and pay respect to Shiva?* But I felt stuck, self-conscious. I was afraid to make a fool of myself by lying down on the floor in full view of the pilgrims.

Immediately, I saw the irony in my thinking: *Here I am, on Mahashivaratri, a day devoted to the God of egolessness, and I'm concerned about what others will think of me if I pray in public? Get over yourself, girl-*

friend. Gingerly, I approached the deity, lowered myself to my knees, and bowed. "Om Namah Shivaya," I whispered, touching my forehead to the cool ground in my own modest version of prostration. When I opened my eyes, arose, and looked around, not a soul was staring at me, of course. It felt right that I had made such a gesture and stepped out of my comfort zone—and my heart was indeed smiling as I took my leave from the main shrine area.

My afternoon wanderings through the temple complex continued to bring magic into my heart and mind. At the promptings of a polite tout, I offered a few rupee coins to a magnificent mama elephant, by way of her snout. I marveled at the horizontal third-eye Shiva markings painted on her forehead, and delighted in gazing into the pachyderm's tiny eyes as she winked at me. As a "reward" for the five-rupee *baksheesh*, she raised her trunk high above my head, curled it into a large "S" shape, and blessed me with a gentle head scruff. Filled with sheer happiness, I sighed audibly with sheer joy, as if I were five years old.

Thinking I'd take my leave from the temple to find a nice *thali* lunch nearby, I made my way toward the exit where I had left my shoes with a watchwoman at the gate. But I was stopped by a sadhu with a small, protruding Buddha belly, watching over a small Shiva lingam temple. He motioned me to come over to join him and his counterpart, a skinny, shaven sadhu in an orange loincloth. Both of them had twinkling eyes, long white hair and beards, and merry smiles. I felt like I'd been summoned by Santa Claus sadhus, albeit with brown skin.

The roly-poly Santa baba blessed me with sandalwood *vibhuti* paste, which is made from the ashes of holy fire. First, he added water to the paste, then smeared it into three straight lines horizontally on my forehead. The design was made complete by a red circular point in the center—just like my elephant friend and thousands of other pilgrims wear to symbolize the third eye of Shiva. Finally, baba topped the paint job off by adding a small red mark to my throat, which I thought appropriate and auspicious, as my throat chakra needed a little boost. The throat, or fifth, chakra rules communication, creativity, and self-expression. I'd been writer's blocked for days, and needed all the opening I could get.

Following this *teeka* marking and blessing, the baba handed me eight yellow marigolds, and instructed me to string them through my hair, like a real Indian woman. (None of this conversation took place in English—it was animation and Tamil language all the way.) Grinning at baba with gratitude, I began haphazardly sticking the flowers into my wash-'n-go 'do-of-the-month: my tresses were pulled up tightly into two small Princess Leah-type buns, and the stems of the blossoms stuck nicely here and there, this way and that way.

Baba was so pleased; he handed me the lid of his stainless steel *tiffin* lunch container to use as a mirror. I peered into the makeshift looking glass. I looked like a cross between Drew Barrymore trying to look cute at the Oscars, and a disheveled hippie. Apparently, the sadhus thought so too. Giggling, the Santas summoned a local woman passerby, asking her to do the job properly. She scurried over and, by pantomime, asked whether I had a comb, which I miraculously had on me, and she set to work.

Out came the flowers. Out came my hair clips and rubber bands. Out came my entire attempt at a floral headpiece. She was determined to make me into a proper Indian woman. She expertly brushed my hair back as she had done for so many sisters and daughters, tied up my half of my hair to let the back fall down my neck, and asked baba for a string, which he instantly produced. With expert skill, she strung up the marigolds into a mini-garland, and wrapped the colorful crown 'round my topknot.

Et voila! Now, replete with floral wreath, Shiva's third eye, and Ganesha's blessings *a la* the elephant showering my spirit—*now* I was ready for Shivaratri!

I expressed my gratitude to the holy men by buying lunch for everyone. For a mere $0.58, four of us (the local man who fetched the lunch joined in, too) ate off large banana leaf fronds, right on the temple steps, perched before the lingam. It was a fine feast, too: *dal*, sweet potatoes, okra "lady fingers," *papadam* lentil chips, rice, buttermilk, pickle relish, and, of course, lots of prayers. The best way to say thank you, hello, goodbye, yes, and any other sentiment to a Shaivite—a follower of Shiva—is quite simple:

"Shiva, Shiva," the babas would say every time they wanted more rice or dal, or said thank you to the server. Simply that: "Shiva, Shiva." "Shiva, Shiva."

Say the name of The One That is All…formlessness, consciousness, destruction and creation…and all will be well.

After lunch, I meditated with the babas for the better part of an hour. I was amazed at how quickly my mind had quieted, how easily I sat, and how peaceful I'd become.

Maybe, just maybe, I have begun to make real peace with Shiva.

Full Circle Celebration

17ᵗʰ of February, Tiruvannamalai

I did it!

On the peak of the New Moon of Mahashivaratri, I joined the throngs of pilgrims here in Tiruvannamalai, as we traversed 'round the sacred mountain of Arunachala, representing Shiva himself in the form of fire. At midnight. Fourteen kilometers. In bare feet!

It was so peaceful, even as thousands of devotees, families, priests and sadhus chanted softly or silently to themselves, and we collectively and contemplatively strode through the night. The mood was bright. People were happy, spending time with their families and loved ones. Mothers carried their babies the entire way. Young children made their way alongside their parents, holding their hands. We stopped at dozens of temples all along, receiving blessings and offering prayers. Chai flowed freely, love filled the air. Most of us wore a soft smile on our lips.

The shared walking meditation was powerful. I marveled at how easy it was to keep a clear, calm mind, bringing my attention back to the focus of honoring India's most revered god, Lord Shiva. It taught me to never underestimate the power of a group in creating a collective consciousness—a force that can be used in so many positive ways.

Today, I'm a little blistered in feet, a lot bolstered in spirit, and up for the next leg of my journey.

Now that I've made peace with Shiva in this holy place—*now* I'm ready for the Andamans!

All aboard!

The Good, the Bad, and the Downright Ugly

25ᵗʰ of February, The Andaman Islands

Whenever one thinks they've nailed down hard travel in India, she throws us another loop-de-loop and a hoop to jump through. I have awarded myself an unofficial "Intrepid Traveler" award. After one hell of a three-day journey, I made it. I'm here, in the Andaman Islands.

With no expectations of what would await me in the islands, I set out from Chennai by ship. A little anxious, a little excited for my first experience putting in hard nautical miles, I climbed aboard our valiant ocean liner: the M.V. Akbar, a "retroactively condemned" ship purportedly on its last legs, or final fins as the case may be.

Turns out, long ago in its heyday, the M.V. ("Moving Vessel") Akbar transported thousands of Muslim pilgrims on a regular basis from Mumbai to Mecca. Now, they keep it alive—just barely—to haul military men and lower-class travelers back and forth from the mainland to the Andamans.

I quite expected the three-day journey to be grueling. I just didn't expect it to be gruesome. Here's a little taste of life on the Akbar—affectionately renamed by me as the "Ack-Barf"—in ultra-budget bunk class:

SQUAT, PISS, SHIT, SNARL

Imagine…hundreds of Indian women *pissing* and *shitting* at, near, or on your feet while you're standing in the sewage collection stinkpot that is the third-class ladies' toilet. You're trying to keep things relatively sanitary as you brush your teeth at the sink. You point out that—with every bit of patience in your snarl—the TOILETS in fact are to be used for excretion purposes, and not the washroom floor. The Indian *didi* retorts viciously, with accompanying haughty head wobble, "You don't eat off the floor, do you?"

Thali for Breakfast, Thali for Lunch, Thali for Dinner

Rice and dal. Dal and rice. Isn't it nice? You can't bear to pick up another grain of pasty-white malnutrition rice, laden with watered-down lentil gruel, with your blackened-under-nails-from-ship-filth-dirty fingers! So you essentially lock down into fasting mode, self-starving for three days. (One of the first things Jan says to me upon our reunification in the islands: "You are less fat now, no?" Ah, yes, the Czech has a way with words.)

The Travelers' Rant

What else are you gonna do on a trans-ocean cesspool, but rant with the wee population of Westerners about how disgusting and horrible the food and the toilets are? Meet three of my favorite fellow foreigners:

Thurston J. Howell III

A British gentleman named Robert, from the south of London, had me in stitches with his lock-jaw drawl, reminiscent of Thurston J. Howell III from *Gilligan's Island*. This well-educated, good-hearted, middle-aged British bloke was spending his days avoiding a regular job at all costs, instead opting to sail the seven seas and fly the friendly skies amongst the more youthful backpacker circuit. His wit and humor were so dry, you'd miss it if it weren't for the fact that he was 90% deaf and had to holler every sentence.

The Belgian Bicyclist

Geert, a mohawk-sporting, biscuit-eating, birdwatching bicyclist from Bruges, had cycled solo across the Indian subcontinent—like Jan.

I wanted to learn more about what makes these eccentric Euro-cyclists tick—maybe discover a little something about what makes Jan's own spokes spin, or something like that—so I chatted up the Flemish chap. Geert entertained us all with tales of traversing West Africa on wheels, keeping us filled up with the cases of biscuits he'd brought aboard to avoid starvation, accompanied with chai from his ever-full camping thermos. Thanks, Geert.

The Grumpy German

Ella, 30, from Munich, was NOT a happy camper. She remained prostrate most of the day on the upper bunk of cracked plastic vinyl opposite my own. It was not a comfortable berth, to say the least. We'd stew away for hours day and night—filthy from ship grime, sweat, and stench—consistently kvetching and complaining. Every time Ella returned from eating, drinking, or using the toilet, off we'd start another round of rag-gin'. Let's just put it this way: I don't think the *M.V. Ack-Barf* was Miss Proper's idea of a proper holiday.

Such was the screenplay and setting for my maiden seafaring voyage. Not quite the Princess Cruise, is it?

Three-days later, we arrived in Port Blair, the capital of The Andaman Islands state. I've never cleared customs and hustled my way out of port so fast—a decontamination shower was in order. I swooped through Port Blair just as fast as my rickshaw-negotiating skills would carry me, hurrying my way out of that hellhole to endure one night in a fleabag ho-tel. Pre-dawn, the morning after the M.V. Akbar's arrival into Port Blair, I ferried over to holiday-maker's Havelock, the most touristy island in the Andaman chain.

The Andamans appear to be a little stretch of paradise, a fine place to rest up before I return to the mainland in a month. Today, I'm dirty, exhausted, and worn from "The Good, The Bad, and The Downright Ugly" ship trip—and as a reward, I'm sitting before some of the most vivid, coral-blue seas I've ever seen. Within a week, I'll be heading to another enchanted isle to rough it up, Robinson Crusoe style. But before I get down like Girl Friday, I need a break, including some yummy beach time, sleep-in time, and snorkel action.

Honey, I'm Home

27th of February, Havelock Island

Upon arriving to Havelock Island, I determined to set out and find the cheapest lodging possible, saving several rupees by taking local buses. Eventually, after walking, walking, walking for several sweaty kilometers—oh, the distance these legs have covered over the last six months!—I found a very happy, affordable option: a honey of a hut in a hippie haven called "Honey Home."

My honeycomb hovel was costlier than any comparable accommodation I've seen on the mainland, but definitely affordable by the islands' tourist mafia standards. Thanks to a tip from a travelin' friend who'd been here a few months ago, I knew to expect exorbitant prices. I chatted the manager down from 250 rupees a night to 200 rupees a night after doing the right thing: ask the Israelis hanging about—the best bargainers on the backpacker circuit—what they are paying, then don't let the boss charge you any more than that.

You get what you bargain for. At this bamboo barrack, there wasn't even a real door—just a few old saris hung over bamboo slats. Though you could lock one bamboo limb to another, security was pretty slim. That said, the setting was absolutely marvelous. The first morn, I awakened at sunrise to the cock-a-doodle-doo of the village roosters, and strolled down to the sea to watch the magnificent change of colors in a nearby mangrove before breakfast. Jaw-dropping beauty!

Nestled in at Honey Home, I thought I'd have a bit of time to myself to rest, beautify, and freshen up after the M.V. Akbar hell-on-sea journey. Several serene days of guitar strumming and solo girl empowering were definitely in order. I needed some serious R 'n R before Jan was to arrive. He'd be appearing in about a week, according to the email I'd received, traveling over from his own camp on Little Andaman Island.

But my coveted week of respite was not to be.

That first long morning, I savored some long-needed primping and preening, tweezing and plucking perched in my hut. It'd been a brutal haul across the Bay of Bengal and a girl must have her occasional beauty treatments. I looked forward to several hours of writing, napping, and relishing, daydreaming and doodling.

Gazing out to sea through the bamboo slats of my non-existent door, he caught my drowsy eye. I stared agape. I couldn't believe it, but there was absolutely no mistaking the tall, lean form hustling across the coconut grove. He was moving fast and sweating profusely, hauling God-knows-how-many kilos of cooking pots and camping gear on his back.

"Jan!" I called out, revealing my location through the non-existent doors. My Czech man turned around on a dime, flashed a happy smile, and threw his gear on the sandy ground. There he was again—just like that—with a twinkle in his blue eyes and a bronze, tanned glow to his skin. He'd been in the wild for over a week. Dirty, dusty, and smelling like hell, he sprinted over to my hut.

I embraced him warmly. Kissed him. Kissed him some more. And as he started to cozy up in my tiny little lair, my newly clean and sparkling girly hut, I pulled back and pointed in the direction of the outdoor shower block. With another kiss and a smile, I firmly directed my jungle man: "Go take a shower."

Of course, we didn't leave the hut for the rest of the day—too much catching up to catch up on. The next day, even though I was still recovering from the boat trip, we were instantly active as per Jan's usual standards: biking fourteen kilometers uphill to the other side of the island. Jan had stored his touring bike in Port Blair, so we rented two bikes, which were miserable excuses for transportation. Being the gentleman, Jan took the less comfy ride, and rode the entire day with a seat spring poking him in the ass. I just prayed on the entire return trip—a steep downhill incline—that my brakes wouldn't give out.

We fell in love with the oh-so-creatively named "Beach Number Seven" on the other side of the island. Jan resolved to return to Beach Number Seven the very next morn and immediately set up camp. He was itching to get back to castaway status lest he lose the Robinson Crusoe groove he'd been in for the past ten days while he'd been waiting for me to show up.

I, on the other hand, had barely hung up my hammock at my little Honey Home goddess boudoir. *Shit!* I fumed. *I gotta haul my ass all the way across the island already? I just got off the damn cargo ship!* Clearly, I wasn't prepared to rough it again so quickly. Still a wee bit of a cosmopolitan camper, perhaps?

But, I know that life is short, and I would sleep when I was eighty, or something like that. So, in alignment with my usual M.O. during travel days with Jan, I motivated.

Communication Breakdown

1ˢᵗ of March, Havelock Island

Two days later, I packed up my hut and slung my guitar over my shoulder to catch the bus over to Beach Number Seven, where Jan was already waiting, having scouted out and set up camp the day before.

At the bus stop, I pulled out my guitar to play for a chai wallah family—just my usual tiny repertoire of three or four plucked-out songs to pass the time. One of the onlookers was a beautiful, twenty-something Indian woman, who was evidently mildly mentally disabled. She sat perched next to me on the little bench while I strummed and hummed my medley of tunes. In between two songs, she looked me dead in the eye, with a silver-gray gaze as faraway and mysterious as the stars in the sky. She pointed at my heart, then my womb, and delivered two words, slowly, matter-of-factly:

"You...mother."

"I...I'm sorry?" I stammered, pretending I didn't hear or comprehend. The teenaged boy observing the scene from across the tea stall piped in, "My sister, she is crazy."

Dazed a bit, I distractedly tuned up my guitar and dove in for another tune, which I offered silently to the mother of music, the goddess Saraswati. Afterward, the "crazy" young woman rose from her perch like a *mummy* rising from the dead. "Thank you," she muttered, and wandered off into the nearby fields, as if in a trance—as nebulous and non-human as she had arrived. *How incredibly odd*, I thought, noticing that the hair on the back of my neck had prickled.

All of a sudden, my bus appeared! There it was, rumbling down the road towards the tea stall, less than fifty meters away. I hadn't even finished my cup of chai, let alone packed up my gear. I was sure to miss it, as Indian buses wait for NO ONE, not women, nor children, nor goats, nor cows… (OK, maybe the cow.)

Acting on auto-pilot, I screeched, "CAN YOU HELP ME???" to the teenaged brother working at the chai shop. The boy bolted from behind the counter, swooped into action, and grabbed my stuff. Off we ran to catch the idling, coughing, beat-up bus wailing warped Hindi music out the grimy windows. The driver was already revving up the engine, itching to leave me behind as I tumbled aboard barely in time.

There are moments traveling where you have to surrender, like entrusting a village boy to be your Insta-Porter and handle your bags on a whim. I didn't even have time to pay the chai wallah ten rupees for my tea, as he waived me away with a head wobble *okay*. I promised him I would find him in a week's time, and pay him with a tip (as I surely did).

Scrunching myself into the bus, I poured into a sea of smiling faces—dozens upon dozens of pigtailed schoolgirls in starched white uniforms with identical red hair bows tied into coconut-oiled plaits. The children were mixed in with a smattering of beach-going Westerners.

At the very next stop, a glowing 'n gorgeous, blond-haired and blue-eyed couple bounded aboard and squeezed in next to me. I couldn't quite place their nationality from their conversing—a guessing-game travelers are wont to play subconsciously—so Curious Erin made small talk. I chirped, "You look like you're ready for a day at the beach!" Smiling, I agreeably wobbled my head at the young woman's super-cute beach tote with pink snorkel and mask poking out. She was wearing chic Ray-Bans, and carried a plastic bag of ripe, luscious mangos.

"Yes, we are!" she chirped right back. I still couldn't place the accent.

German? No. Dutch? No. Hmm... guess I better resort to more advanced tactics. I took the direct route: "Where are you from?" I asked.

"We're from Czech Republic!" she replied with gusto. The couple, who introduced themselves to me as Lenku and Tomas, explained they were on their way to deliver said-ripe-and-luscious mangos to another Czech on Beach Number Seven, whom they had met the day prior. "Is his name Jan?" I asked. "Oh yes! You know him?!" "Yes," I said, "I'm heading there, too. Jan's my boyfriend." Lenku and Tomas informed me that Jan was awaiting us all in his Pláž Paradise camp.

Once we got to Beach Number Seven, the four of us spent a few days together as a team. I was happy for Jan: he must have been thrilled to befriend some fellow Praguians so he could relax in his own language a bit. However, I began to feel frustrated and bordered on bored as I could not understand a damned thing the Slavs were saying. I kept an open mind and a positive attitude, even as Led Zeppelin's "Communication Breakdown" quickly became our camp theme song.

Before we'd said our goodbyes on the mainland last month, Jan had painted a picture of our time on the Andamans as some sort of paradise, in which he would focus on keeping a cozy camp, and I could while away the hours wistfully writing, practicing asana, and learning guitar.

NOT. The first few days of our "Back to Nature" experiment in remote island living, I wanted nothing more than to sit on my ass, to be honest. Frankly, after the Ack-Barf trip, I needed a righteous rest. But by Day Three, Jan had enough of my apparent freeloading, and said, as sweetly and unfazed as he could possibly muster, "You know, Erin, it's sort of nice when the people share a little bit of the work in a camp. Maybe you could at least get firewood while I start cooking."

My first thought: *You mean to tell me we're gonna be living some sort of primal* Quest for Fire *experiment here? I came to do yoga and get a tan.*

My second thought: *I'll show him!*

Like a trooper and proper teammate, I stuck to the second thought and set to work, collecting wood, keeping coals, and fanning flames.

Taken Under

2nd of March, Havelock Island

I got my first taste of being taken under in the islands, just as we were leaving the prime-snorkel-spot of Havelock at Elephant Beach. After a day of coral reef exploration with the Czech couple, Tomas and Lenku, we had to get back to the main road—quickly. Nightfall threatened as we tried to find our way, slogging through a mangrove and hesitantly tiptoeing through the puddles. Trying to cross a stagnant expanse of swamp, I stepped into what appeared to be a two-inch-deep pool of muddy water. *Uh-oh.* The moment my feet plunged into the murky muck, I knew something was wrong. I'd been engulfed by some odd Andamanese form of quicksand!

Instantly, I was calf-high in sludgy, leech- and mollusk-ridden brown goo—and going down fast. My toes went *squish squash*, and I looked down to see hundreds of black mollusks surrounding my legs, which were quickly sinking in the syrupy substance. Coming up behind me, Jan quickly grabbed my arms and pulled me out like I was drowning in molasses, with the vise-grip of vile substance clinging on, blowing out both my flip-flops in the process.

Squishy in my destroyed sandals, the four of us made for a hard haul up the jungle slope as darkness descended. We were in a race against time, as the exotic nocturnal creatures began their night calls.

I trailed behind the three spirited Slavs who had proper footwear and were happy as clams. The gorgeous blonde, Lenku, seemed to me to be floating and bouncing gaily over trees and puddles, hardly sweating and never stumbling.

In that moment, I hated them. All of them. *How much longer can I do this?* I asked myself. Rough and thrashed, thrashed and rough. Such was my physical, mental, and emotional state after one week in the relatively tame jungles of Havelock. It was only the beginning.

Finally, after several kilometers walk, we made it back to Beach Seven and, completely done-in from the day, called it a night. I buried myself in my hammock nest and crashed out. In the middle of the night, I awakened from a deep sleep during the Witching Hour, to absorb the lunar rays and experience the magic of a lunar eclipse. I offered up a small prayer for strength to *Chandra*, the mystical Moon, before slipping back into my exhausted slumber.

Heavenly Holi

4ᵗʰ of March, Havelock Island

The next morning after the quicksand incident, Jan and I said good-bye to our driftwood digs on Beach Seven and took off to catch the ferry for the next leg of our Andamanese Magical Mystery Tour. On the way to the bus stop, we ran smack dab in the middle of Holi celebrations!

The Full Moon festival of Holi celebrates the colors and vitality of spring, and the blessings of Lord Krishna. Beauty is everywhere, created by showering each other with vibrant paints and powdered colors. Children, tourists, merchants, priests, mothers, grannies—no one, but *no one* is immune from the paint and play.

Jan and I fell seamlessly into the ruckus, playing full-out with huge smiles in our hearts, pummeling each other with powder and colored-water balloons. We hooted and hollered, laughingly layering color after color on each other and anyone that moved. Even the village goats and month-old kittens were plastered with paint.

Waiting for the ferry to Neil Island, the Holi play was still going strong. The ferry was hours late as usual, so after downing several cups of chai, I pulled out my guitar in a makeshift playground near the jetty. Indians are a forgiving audience for an amateur musician—and Indian *kids* are an *appreciative* audience for an amateur musician. Everyone was in a celebratory mood at the jetty park. The children swarmed around me, giggling, clapping, ogling and laughing along with my songs. They smeared me with oodles of wet powders as I strummed and sang. I looked like a spumoni ice cream sundae!

This is why I lug my instrument around! I thought. These moments of pure, unbridled joy are what I came to India for! I felt my heart crack open even wider, and ran off behind Jan to catch the ferry to Neil Island.

Octopus's Garden

11th of March, Neil Island

All I wanted was a shower.

Or at least a clean pair of underwear.

You know. The little things.

Our Andaman adventure was getting riper by the day. Hence the sincere need for a shower. But that would be a long time in coming.

Once we got off the ferry that transported us from Havelock, Jan and I schlepped our gear several kilometers deeper into the heart of our second jungle, heading to an isolated, picturesque stretch of beach on Neil Island.

I was a bit frazzled in nerves, and the discomfort I felt played out in the relationship zone. A little crabby, perhaps? More than a little. I've never quibbled with a travel partner so very much as the time spent in the Andamans with Jan. There's something about the hardships of backpacking with a new boyfriend in a developing country. It tests our meddle. It summons the best in us, out of necessity and moments of shared triumph and exhilaration; AND the worst in us, out of discomfort and physical and mental taxation.

Add to that a total, forced surrender into survival mode, thrusting yourself into shipwrecked status like a *Lost* or *Survivor* drama, and you've got a setup for explosions of volcanic proportions. Wondering where your weak spots are? You'll find out. Every button you've ever had is raised, just asking to be pushed, prodded, and poked. This is where patience comes in. Patience, and shifting into a completely different mindset than the one you're used to.

I decided to make this time on the islands into a personal experiment. How balanced can I keep my mind, even while feeling totally off-kilter much of the time? In hindsight, I have to give myself a huge pat on the back. No, make that a flippin' gold medal.

Embittered and lacking confidence in my ability to play the part of Miss Family Robinson, I began my time on Neil Island in a sour mood. Luckily, I quickly grew tired of my own whining and wallowing in my emotional cesspool and opted to pray for help: "Please, India, let me be strong! If you want me to leave, show me the way home. If you want me to stay, I pray, grant me strength, and grant it now, lest I lose my only two remaining marbles."

Prayer worked! I woke up the next morning with firm resolve in my heart to keep my chin up. If I hoped to have any fun, not to mention keep flailing sanity intact, I'd need to transform into a Jungle Jane to match Jan's Tarzan game.

So kick into gear I did, once again surrendering to island life with great gusto. Sometimes, the only way out is through.

In spite of my own internal difficulties and the external rows, Jan and I were blessed to scout out and find a nice slice of paradise on Neil Island—a joyful jungle nest we affectionately named "The Octopus's Garden."

"I'd like to be under the sea, in an octopus's garden in the shade." Indeed, The Beatles' *Abbey Road* was our shared soundtrack, and Ringo's quirky little ditty suited our home just perfectly—an Octopus's Garden of Eden in a cleared-out palm shelter just off the beach. The Garden was, in my opinion, the nicest camp we made in the islands. Jan was truly in his element, living out his long-cherished fantasy of the Ultimate Andaman Experience. I was getting stronger too. By this point, my dusted-off camping skills were becoming nicely honed.

Mornings were marked, Aquarian Water Bearer that I am, by stealthily snagging our day's water from a vegetable farmer's nearby well. Catching me hauling up the bucket the very first morning, the old man gave me a head wobble in approval, so we were good to go in the hydration department. We also had no qualms about drinking the well water—our immune systems were surely stable and steely by this point. Plus, empty packets of pesticide were strewn about the well's stone wall perimeter. Hardcore as we were, we figured, A*in't nothing gonna live in that water— there isn't a microbe left with all these chemicals nearby.* Toxic, but true. You'll do what you can to stay alive in the wild.

Living in such ideal surroundings gave us both more energy to get creative. We played chess in the sand, with figures made of seashells. Knights, rooks, pawns, queens and all—represented by abandoned crustacean homes, found right in our front yard.

We also made some of our best grub in The Octopus's Garden. Jan built a harpoon from found objects, including the filed-down handle from my stainless steel spoon. Donning diving mask and snorkel, Jan speared two fish within twenty minutes. Clearly, his scout years as a youth in Communist Czechoslovakia were paying off in spears.

Together, Jan and I prepared scrumptious fish tacos for dinner, fashioning tortillas out of campfire-cooked chapatis, topped off with lime and cilantro. Life in The Garden was truly divine.

Garden of Eden

13th of March, Neil Island

After a week on Neil Island, I had really begun to hit my stride—wood-hauling, *masala* chai-making, water-bearing, and more. I'd long since given up on the idea of a proper shower, opting instead to plunge into the surf whenever I felt a bit gamey. Honestly, at this point, I didn't notice—and I most certainly didn't care.

Jan and I were having such a good time, I wanted to play and stay in the Octopus's Garden for many more a day. But, we were scheduled to depart the next morning for our final destination, Long Island. Since the ferries ran only twice a week, we had to get moving and pack up.

In honor of our last full day in The Garden, as Shakti paying homage to her consort Shiva, I offered Jan a strand of sacred beads, called *Rudraksha*, known as "Shiva tears." I had purchased the mala in the Tiruvannamalai Shiva temple, as a remembrance of my beautiful night of Maha Shivaratri. Jan gave me a thank you kiss and promptly donned the mala, wrapping the gift around his wrist. In a loving mood, we set out to enjoy a romantic last evening by our cozy campfire.

Jan was, by default, the leader of the camp when it came to the day-to-day details, and he often assumed a teaching role when it came to the art of surviving so far off the beaten path. He made a special point to learn a few things from me as well—things like sun salutations, really-really-strong-coffee-making, and other useful skills.

Tonight, our last night in the Garden, Jan was keen on learning something else from me. Jan was interested in tantra.

"Really?" I asked him. "*You*, Mr. Non-Spiritual, are interested in tantra? You're not just mocking me?" I knew Jan well enough by now. If something smacked remotely mystical, he wouldn't take it seriously, which was one of the biggest chasms in our communication.

"Yes, show me tantra," he assured me with a playful gleam in his eye, like any good Gemini.

So I began, talking into the late evening. I shared with Jan the tiny bit I know about tantra, carefully pointing out that it is much more vast and mysterious than most of us can even begin to understand, and I had hardly any personal experience with it. I readily clarified that, while I don't know much, I *do* know that it is an art that must be taken sincerely and seriously, for powerful energies are awakened upon its practice. Sex is hardly a fraction of the foundation.

"It is said," I explained to Jan, "that the Kundalini serpent goddess, coiled at the base of the spine, is aroused and awakened through tantric practices. I do know one basic tantric exercise we can try, if we both agree to keep an open heart and an open mind. It's called *yab-yum*, where the female sits astride the male—like this." I demonstrated, sitting on Jan's lap and wrapping my legs around him. "It's actually a meditation position evoking perfect, divine balance between Shiva and Shakti."

Fully at attention, Jan was, of course, up for it. And if this were a Bollywood film, we'd cut away at this point to a song and dance in fields of grass. You get the picture.

Taking the tantric invocation to heart, I prayed to Shiva and Shakti to manifest through us, through our devotion to each other in an act of sacred sex. As the last candle flickered and the campfire flames died down, we lingered a bit longer, stretched out on our straw mat on the ground. Content, I made myself comfy and cozy, to lay and gaze up at the jungle canopy just a few moments more.

And then, I heard Her—the goddess Kundalini who was indeed awakened, and manifest here and NOW.

Hiss-s-s-s-s-s-s-s-s-s-s...

Glancing to my right, not two feet from where we lay stark naked on the ground, was the longest, scariest serpent I've ever come face to face with. She was slithering her way out of the jungle foliage and into our Garden, moving slowly but steadily in our direction.

S-s-s-s-s-s-s-s-s-s-s...

I lurched up from the mat to get the hell out of the way, catapulting instantly in an adrenalin-filled, side-flip superhero move that launched me several feet across the camp into my hammock.

Jan hadn't noticed her. "What is it?" he asked. Firmly, under trembling breath, I warned, "SNAKE! SNAKE!" Jan leaped up and bolted backward.

She was at least two meters long, with thick stripes of alternating shades of light and dark green, looking very poisonous—this was no sweet sea snake. I noticed every detail of her tiny tongue darting rapidly in and out, and she was moving deliberately in our direction.

The serpent slithered through our camp, knocking over our last lit candle with her trailing tale. The candle continued to burn, threatening to catch the straw mat on fire. Jan jumped into gear with a manly-man approach to handling the herptile, attempting to coax her out of camp with a stick. As he stabbed the air with his spear, the Shaivite serpent dramatically raised half her body high in the air, poising as if to strike.

"Oh my God, Jan. Do NOT piss her off!" I pleaded.

Granted, I was hiding out in my hammock, so it was easy for me to say. To his credit, Jan was concerned that the camp would catch on fire from the fallen candle; or, that the candle would indeed go out, and we wouldn't be able to see the snake, which could be even worse.

She nosed around and traversed every corner of our camp, inch by inch. She lingered a while near our campfire embers. Then, for a freaky sort of encore, the serpent actually slithered up to and coiled herself around a massive seashell that, earlier that day, we had filled with dozens of "Shiva's eyes." Every morning in the Andamans, Jan and I would collect handfuls of round, flat shells, called "Shiva's eyes," with natural nautilus-spiral designs that symbolize the third eye as well as protection and positive energy. The Kundalini serpent seemed to like them, too. She would not leave until *She* wanted to leave.

Jan was still standing poised with spear like a naked jungle warrior. "Please, Jan, just let her pass." Naked and shivering, I crouched in my hammock, in mid-air, feeling as if I were staring death in the face. *I could die, or Jan could die,* I thought. *But, if I do die, I can definitely say that I have* lived—*truly, deeply, and fully* lived.

A reassuring thought anyways. It was scary as hell, and yet I was oddly calm. Perhaps I was in shock. Or that age-old survival mode had kicked in. I'm reminded of so many times in India—whether praying for my life on a fishtailing bus skirting cliffs in the Himalayas, or nearly deteriorating from sheer loneliness—where I've felt at or near the brink of death, if even psychologically. There's an eerie, otherworldly calm that sets in at times like this. The witnessing mind takes over. And that's what happened here.

We had to wait for another few minutes for the serpent to pass, on her own accord, in her own sweet time. She made her way in my direction, toward the hammock. Finally, ever so slowly and stealthily, she slithered toward the other side of the jungle…

…directly under my body.

Heart beating heavily, as the snake moved under me, I prayed to high heaven the hammock ropes would hold. The months of sand and sea spray had begun to rot the ropes, and we had experienced more than one bout of unexpected hammock-crashing-to-the-jungle-floor in the night. It was a moment of faith—one of those times when the veil separating life and Mother Nature's virtual death is so thin, you're at the brink of your personal bardo. And all you can do is breathe.

Yes, our seemingly-benign tantric experiment had worked. The Shakti had indeed risen. The visit from the serpent-sister was, for me, a direct representation of consciousness arising in reality. Our coiled Kundalini cobra confirmed to me that the cosmic fire beneath my feet was pulsing vibrantly in these wildly remote, dangerous, and deceptively-beautiful islands.

Jan and I finally agreed on something at last: clearly, it was high time to leave The Octopus's Garden of Eden.

Terms of Endurement

20ᵗʰ of March, Long Island

Enjoy when you can, and endure when you must. ~ Goethe

Buoyed by the beauty and toughened by snakes in The Octopus's Garden of Eden, I thought I'd be well-prepared for the trials and tribulations awaiting me at our next destination, Long Island. Hopping off the ferry, it was getting late and already dark, and the beach where we planned on camping was a minimum two-hour hike through the jungle. We couldn't have gotten off to our camp on time anyway, as Jan and I were ordered by the island constable to register our passports and Andaman permits at the police station.

We obeyed and—along with a handful of other hard-core backpackers—schlepped our stuff from the jetty over to the village, filled out the paperwork, and asked the sari-adorned station agent where the nearest guest house might be located.

"No guest house on island," she said with a toothy smile and a clinking of bangles.

So, our first night on Long Island, Jan and I bedded down right smack dab in the middle of the village, in the cricket playground. Talk about flexible. I lay down my straw mat and snuggled into my sleeping bag—after shaking it inside out first, checking for snakes and spiders—and stared at the stars.

I was *so* tired. Not just physically. My soul was tired. After almost five months of hard traveling, I simply didn't find camping on a cricket ground to be the most comforting. It's also about the people that you're with. I needed my friends. Sure, I was with Jan—someone I was relatively close to—but he wasn't a long-time member of my *tribe*, you know? I needed to talk to a girlfriend, a confidante, a therapist! Someone I could VENT to. Someone who could understand I wanted a bikini wax, a cup of non-Nescafé instant coffee, a proper BED, for crying out loud. I lulled myself to sleep with promises of future good coffee ("Someday, you'll have espresso!").

Next morning, we went straight to work, hustling and bustling to get a week's worth of food supplies together. Jan bargained for a machete to crack open coconuts while I stocked up on coconut oil, *nag champa* incense, and mosquito repellent. Long Island was to be the grand finale of our Andaman Crusoe experience. Jan was living out his fantasy, his Long-Island-awaited castaway dream. I, on the other hand, was cast somewhere between *The Blue Lagoon* and a complete loon.

Spilling over with sacks of lentils, rice, bananas, chai fixings, and chapati flour, we gave our backs a break and splurged for a shortcut to the beach: a half-dozen of us Westerners hired a flimflam boatman and his little brother to putter us over to Lalaji Beach, supposedly the *crème de la crème* paradisiacal find in all the Andamans.

The rickety boat dumped us off on the shore, threw our backpacks overboard, and the batch of us weary travelers scattered in various directions to find camping spots. After searching for a good hour, Jan and I came across a pre-scouted campsite of fallen logs and readymade fire pit, directly located on the white sandy beach, with the gorgeous backdrop of a coconut plantation. The turquoise, crystal-clear sea was our front yard. A pristine well was a five-minute walk. And, we weren't in the middle of the jungle foliage.

Oh goodie! No massive crabs crunching through our camp all night. And no sneaky serpents slithering through, either. We thought we'd scored. Something in the back of my mind said, "Hmmm. This is odd. If this is such an ideal location to camp, why is it empty? Why aren't any other backpackers around?" My intuition told me something would be not quite right, but I would find that out later—once I had ignored my intuition, which my intuition says is never a good thing to do.

Chalking our perfect campsite up to Lady Luck, Jan and I got busy and built up our third and final home on the Andaman Islands. We set up a top-notch kitchen, and created captivating curries, breakfast *kheer* rice pudding with coconut milk, dried fruits and cashews. It was all topped off with the perfect masala chai black tea with cardamom, cinnamon, and heaping helpings of fresh ginger.

The highlight of my island life: exquisite yoga in the coconut planta- tion, which was our backyard. It was my little moment to shine, teaching Jan the beauty of hatha yoga. Each morning, we kept our commitment to shared practice, stirring at dawn and diving into the gifts of *asana*. Exploring the intricacies of a single pose—whether shoulder stand, or downward dog, or simple sitting in breathing meditation—held as much joy and fulfillment as any other travel adventure.

Each day, we added another round of *Surya Namaskar* sun salutations to our practice, feeling our breath capacity, spine strength, and flexibility increase with each cycle. Together, we felt a synergy unfold—the ulti- mate union of yin and yang.

But, after a few days, we discovered why there were no other travelers nearby, why no others had snagged our campsite. Why no one, but *no one* else was to be seen in our general vicinity.

Sand fleas.

Sounds relatively harmless. Sounds like, oh, a few bites here and there. A few nagging itches, right?

Wrong. Let's just say I now have *tremendous* compassion for our feline and canine companions. Allow me to describe the following state of mis- ery for your edification:

Suffering all night long in my hammock, trying without success to avoid scratching, which is about as futile as instructing a toddler to refrain from scratching chicken pox. I am in mental and physical agony, raging like a banshee on fire. At the very first hint of dawn, I hurl myself out of the hammock, tear off every stitch of clothing, and run naked and crying into the sea. Standing neck-deep in the surf, I am boiling with frustration and rage. The water is the only place I can be in any comfort. I could give a flying fig whether the fishermen collecting their nets nearby can see me in my birthday suit, and I let out a wail that would make your skin crawl. The beauty of the turquoise, crystalline waters set against the backdrop of a pristine pink and purple sunrise, the irony of this scene, makes it all the worse, and torrents of tears roll down my cheeks in sheer helplessness.

We tried every solution to stop the itching and quell the maddening malady: coconut oil, *Navratna* oil (an ayurvedic panacea, touted as being good for everything from impotency to sleeplessness to hair loss, but apparently failing in the flea department), Tiger Balm, antiseptic ointment...Even, at the advice of a sweet-natured Swedish hippie girl, tamari soy sauce. Anything, but anything to soothe the agony. I didn't even care that I smelled like a shish kebab.

Who would have thought that a tiny little black insect, the size of a pinhead, could wreak such havoc? Jan was incredibly uncomfortable, too. I was truly at wit's end. I needed someone, something to airlift me out of this misery. The next night of hell, instead of hanging in my hammock and counting the hours for dawn to come so I could plunge into the pacifying surf, I got up in the dark, went solo to the waterside, held my head in my hands, and bitched to the Bay of Bengal.

It was the darkest night of my life. Except for the soft sounds of the waves lapping against the shore, it was dead silent. I looked up at the ink-black sky. I had never seen so many stars. The half-Moon stared down upon me without emotion, seemingly mocking me. For the first time during my travels, she offered me no solace. Only emptiness. Nothingness.

I prayed, but there was no god or goddess there for me in that moment. Only a billion steely stars in the vastness. I couldn't appreciate Nature's beauty. Instead, I was wallowing in ugliness and harshness.

At that moment, the only thing that kept me going was faith. At that moment, the practices I'd worked with in the West surfaced from my soul to get me through—the sayings and parables that sound cliché when you hear them, but damn straight, they will get you through when the going gets tough. Teachings of impermanence, sayings like *This too shall pass,* or *This will also change.*

The loneliness and despair was incomparable. Sure, Jan was being a good and fair team player, doing his best to take care. But we'd only been together for two months, and it hadn't been the rosiest road. More than anything, I wished I could beam one of my best friends over to that remote island. Someone who knows me, you know? *Really* knows me. In that night of complete and total darkness and emptiness, all I wanted was someone close to be there, to hold my hand, and tell me, "It's going to be okay, Erin. It's really going to be okay."

And in some way, my dearest friends *were* there. Because I thought of them, and they were there.

And dawn came.

The Tides They Are A-Turnin'

27ᵗʰ of March, Bay of Bengal

Without a doubt, my month on the Andaman Islands turned out to be one of the most physically and mentally grueling experiences of my life. I felt as if I were playing a role in Dante's *Inferno*, or living a part of the Persephone myth, having been held captive in some sort of underworld. Definitely ready for some divine springtime, let me tell you.

Jan had to legally leave the islands as his Andaman's permit was expiring. I deliberated briefly as to whether to extend my own stay for another two weeks, with the hopes that an elusive tropical holiday was just around the corner. Maybe, just maybe, I'd bid bon voyage to my boyfriend, my partner in time, and stick around solo for some sort of sun-soaked miracle.

But no matter how hard I tried, I simply could not envision these islands embracing me. In fact, they were kicking me out the door. In one sense, the Andamans are so wild, so very untamed—it's as if Mother Nature herself gives you the boot in order to preserve herself as long as possible.

And besides, how long can one endure the hell realm, the absence of solace and light, right?

From crunching crabs and slithering snakes and infuriating fleas, from coral-cuts and scarred shins, and middle-of-night hammocks hurling to the jungle floor—it's not a difficult question.

I decided I'd had enough of hell. It was time to get back to the mainland, back to the Divine Comedy of life in civilization. Jan and I bought our tickets for the long ship journey back to Calcutta, fortuitously set to arrive on the spring equinox.

Our vessel, the Good Ship M.V. Nicobar, turned out to be an absolute luxury liner compared to the M.V. *AckBarf.*

I'd heard rumors that the Nicobar was indeed an upgrade, but I wasn't buying it until we actually boarded the boat. In Port Blair for two days before departure, I mentally prepared for the four-day haul. I swore I'd be a breatharian and live off pure ether, rather than attempt to stomach such filthy freight-liner food again.

Jan pledged to help me out of scurvy survival, and the morning of our boarding, we hustled around the fruit and veg markets, picking up stores of tomatoes, cucumber, and lemon for salads, nuts for protein, biscuits and Nescafe for sanity, and an entire branch of bananas, straight off the tree.

Serving as our own sherpas, we hauled all these goods up the loading plank of the ship. Along with our usual load of backpacks, bicycle, panniers, and guitar, we now included twelve whole kilos of bananas— still attached to their original bough. Even the home-cooking Indians thought that was a little extreme, bringing an entire banana tree with us. We were clearly the laughing *stalk.*

I didn't care. We strung our fruity loot above my head in the lower bunk, hanging the banana branch like a baby in a basinet, and concealed the goods with a *lungi.* Every few hours, when hunger kicked in, we'd snag a few single bananas off the branch and have a feast, just like Hanuman, the monkey god.

Lucky for me, on this return journey to the mainland, I had a plucky pioneer to help ease the discomfort. Jan is one of the most courageous adventurers I've ever known—as he would need to be, to bicycle from Czech Republic all the way to India, overland. When it comes to intrepid travel, he knows how to make due in the worst of conditions.

Being a natural extrovert and "people person," I had a grace and finesse in building an instant community with other Westerners. But when it came to initiating contact with the local Indians, Jan is extraordinary. It's partly because of his Central European good looks—the blue eyes and height alone catch the Indians' attention; he stands out, commanding a certain respect from the Indians, perhaps out of curiosity or out of wonder. Like it or not, the Indians also gave him automatic respect because he is a male. Also, his blatant assertiveness opened doors.

Take, for example, navigating the ship. This vessel was HUGE, a virtual floating city. I couldn't get from Point A to Point B without losing myself along the way. Every time I'd go from the lower—a-hem—bowels of the ship, where our third class bunks were located, and try to make my way to the upper deck where we'd hang out with the other travelers, I'd take several wrong turns, just like a maze. I definitely got my exercise, going round and round, up and down, lost on several flights of steps, leading to dead-ends, purser's chambers, and captain's quarters.

But within ten minutes of hopping on board, while I was still stringing up the banana bassinet in my bunk, Jan had scouted out the old, yellowing diagrams of the ship's layout posted by the information booth. Instantly, Inspector Jan had figured out when the lending library was open, how to get to the galley, and what time the old Bruce Lee flick—in Hindi!—was showing in the Bunk Class Rec Room.

I was glad he knew about the kitchen, that's for sure. Knowing my terror at the *thali* meals awaiting us for breakfast, lunch, and dinner, Jan took me by the hand and showed me the secret backdoor to the galley. Then he instructed me, "You know how to do it. Turn on that smile."

I peered in through the porthole windows in the doors. I could see the Indian cooks in there, preparing the evening meal. To my glee, everything was clean, clean, clean. Where I had seen filth and dirt in the M.V. Ackbar kitchen, with whole chickens carcasses lying on the dirty floor behind the canteen counter, the Nicobar galley exuded lovely scents of simmering curries. Fresh vegetables were chopped up and thrown into massive vats and pots, and the cooks were smiling and chatting away.

I opened the swinging doors and introduced myself with a cheery "Hello!" The gracious all-male staff of cooks looked up from their tasks and immediately greeted me with pleasantries, offering to fill up my bottle with hot *pani* for my instant coffee. "Anything you need, Madame, anytime. Welcome to our kitchen!"

What a relief! Jan and I enjoyed sunsets on the deck, munching biscuits and chugging chai and Nescafe. I relished in a sense of safety on this ship, a pleasant aura of protection. With Jan at my side, I could actually *enjoy* the scenery too, without being hassled too much. We'd play chess on our travel set for hours on end—so much fun for us both, since in the West, one rarely takes the time to play the game of such study and concentration. I even read a whole book without having to fend off incessant stares or irritating questions like "Which country?" and "Married?"

Jan and I befriended a sweet Spanish señorita, Monica, who had mastered a mean flamenco. The three of us mapped out a "chill zone"—two words understood by young people the world over—which quickly became the place to hang for the twenty-two western travelers aboard. Yoga mats were laid down, blankets, biscuits and drums emerged. Over the next four days, tall traveling tales and stories were shared, and fast friendships were formed.

Now *this* was what I was looking for. Forget isles of isolation. I needed a sense of *community*! Now we were in my territory—the realm of humanity and socialization. I felt reconnected in the most delightful of ways, as the first rays of spring shone down upon us, and we rode the last waves into the docks at sunset. Calcutta, the city of the Divine Mother Kali herself, welcomed us with open arms and played heavenly hostess for a magnificent first evening.

Every single one of us—especially the thirstier Irish and Brits in the bunch—clamored for an icy cold one. We were already punch drunk, worn and weary from our four-day schooner journey. No matter. Our backpacking bunch scurried off to find rooms in the travelers' hovel—the Sudder Street slum.

First priority: shower as fast as possible. After taking half a bottle just to get a lather going in my hair—indeed, it had been over three weeks before shampoo and fresh water had graced my gritty locks—I had been reincarnated as a something resembling a human being. It was impossible to get more than the surface layer of dirt off in one round, and Jan was impatient for a beer, so I told myself the entire next day would be devoted to beauty.

But now: we drink. Just like any sailors who'd just rolled into port, the whole crew of us met up minutes later at the closest watering hole.

What amazing people! A global representation: Belgian, Israeli, American, Czech, Aussie, Irish, British, Indian, German, Polish, Spanish, and Swiss—the giddy group joined together for a gala evening of celebration. Blowing off steam and stress, we topped it all off with a night of cutting the rug in a posh hotel discotheque.

As far and wide as I love to travel, I could not have been happier to be back on the mainland. And as wild and crazy, unpredictable and chaotic as Calcutta may be, I was utterly thrilled to be back in the cosmopolitan groove of civilization. I boogied and bounced to bad disco into the wee hours, and thanked my lucky stars.

It felt so good—so very, very good—to be alive.

In the Arms of the Mother

29ᵗʰ of March, Kolkata

I was shocked from the outset in Kolkata, and in a completely opposite way than expected. From my associations of poverty, leprosy, and
squalor—Mother Teresa's Home for the Dying, LaPierre's *City of Joy*, and
the acclaimed documentary *Born Into Brothels*, for example—I thought
I'd be running for cover or cowering fearfully in my hotel room.

Quite the contrary. Calcutta took my breath away. From Day One,
after sleeping off our night of disco-dancing-'til-dawn, Jan and I plunged
into the capital city of West Bengal, immersing ourselves in the city street
life. We reveled in the fascinating mix of degradation and dilapidation,
contemporary culture, aesthetics and art. We lost ourselves in the most
pleasant of ways, far off the beaten tourist track, wandering into 'hoods
and hovels, encountering Indian eyes that rarely, if ever, had ogled such
pale skin. By this point in my travels, I was so comfortable with contrast
that I embraced it, practically sought it out.

Sometimes, we'd give the slum kids a few coins, treat a beggar for tea,
or buy an extra curd *lassi* for a leper child. Often, we just gave them the
simple gift of acknowledging their existence and humanity, and a few
moments of our time. I watched—and learned—as Jan playfully, fearlessly bantered with the beggar children. When a grubby gutter urchin

would rush up to me, pleading for rupees or "just one chocolate," I could actually hold their hand now, and walk with them down the alleyways. The love and hunger would pour forth from their imploring eyes, spilling into my heart until it overflowed as nectar, and back to them through the squeeze of my hand grasp. I was beginning to comprehend the incomprehensible in Kali's own city, in the arms of the Mother.

Catalyst for Change

30ᵗʰ of March, Kolkata

Although, like everything in India, the origins are controversial, most people accept that the name Kolkata, or Calcutta, is derived from one of its colonial central villages, called "Kalikata" or "Kalikshetra," meaning, "Land of the goddess Kali."

Who is this Mother Kali? Why does she enrapture me? Why, in heaven's name, would I intertwine myself with a wrathful devi, who inhabits the cremation grounds? The Divine Mother in the form of the fierce Ma Kali came to me in a vision. At first, I couldn't accept this form of the Mother—red blood dripping from her lolling tongue, jet-black tresses flying wildly, naked save for a garland of decapitated heads and belt of human arms, brandishing sword, sickle, and skulls from her arms. But, since she appeared while I was meditating, though I was frightened at first, I decided to get to know her better. Besides, I believe that we judge that which we do not understand—so I strove for better understanding.

Through my research, I learned that Kali is anything but evil. *Kali*, which also means "black" and "She Who is Time," is a force of nature that fully embraces death as a part of life. She doesn't run from darkness—she devours it, and thereby transforms darkness into light. She is the Divine Slayer of Illusion, assisting us in cutting away whatever thoughts, attitudes, or beliefs stand in our way. Her fierce likeness—

whether seen as an archetype of the collective unconscious, or as a very real, down-to-earth incarnation of Shakti—is a constant reminder of the only constant: change.

Kali, like her divine consort Shiva, is both creator and destroyer—a timeless, never-ending figure eight, the infinite cycle of life. To reject this truth is, in essence, to reject the truth of nature. The harvest of late summer, the decomposition of autumn, the incubation period of winter all precede the new growth of spring, where we resurrect again and again.

No doubt, after just a few short days in Calcutta, I would hear my own call for quick change. The mother of creation and transformation herself had already started with a few sharp, significant pricks, indicating it was high time to get a move on.

"Go West, Young Woman!"

30ᵗʰ of March, Kolkata

I was so in love with life in Calcutta that I wanted to stay in her cozy arms for a long, long time—even after Jan said goodbye, setting out across north India en route to Delhi.

I would miss him—how could you go through something so intense with another person without them becoming a part of your very soul?

Yet, I knew we had to go our separate ways. Even if we had endured so much together, and learned so much from each other, we were NOT meant to be a couple. Friends, yes. Partners? No way. We loved each other and cared a great deal for each other, but we were not compatible—we argued all the time, about stupid and petty things that shouldn't matter. We seemed to take away from each other's happiness rather than contribute. So, in lieu of starting to really despise each other, we cut our losses and said goodbye.

I'll never forget watching him ride off on his bicycle into Kolkata's burnt-orange setting sun, toward Bihar. Jan promised he would get me a leaf from the bodhi tree in Bodh Gaya, and I knew he would—because that's the kind of friend Jan is. After saying goodbye, I sat myself down and thought about my options and what I would do, where I would go next.

I had quickly grown comfortable in Calcutta. Our room in the Salvation Army guest house was a dank, decrepit dungeon, but I dug it in some weird way. Our nearby 'hood included a park, metro station, market, theater, and cheap Internet. I could write here, work here! I'd made the acquaintance of a few well-educated, inviting local women, including one of the top designers in West Bengal. The Manhattan-y mystique of cabs, chaos, and culture was creatively stimulating. I didn't even seem to mind the fact that it was a three-shower-a-day kind of humidity.

I could *feel* that my karma was quickening, my time in India was finishing. Still, I had a scheme up my sleeve to stay. And you know what they say about schemes: "If you want to make the gods laugh, tell 'em your plans."

One day, I strolled confidently into the Foreign Registration Office, brandishing my ten-year India visa like a badge of honor pasted in my passport, banking on my Great American Charm to move mountains. Instead, I encountered a five-foot mountain of strewn paperwork, forming a barricade behind which perched a bespectacled bureaucrat who looked as dusty as the piles of files behind him.

"Sorry, madame. You must leave India," he said flatly, without emotion.

"But, sir, it says right here on the TEN-YEAR visa, 'Not to exceed six months without registration.' So, here I am, ready to register!" I stood there nice 'n tall, grinning widely, doing my best to exude confidence that *of course* the answer was *the way* I *planned.*

"Madame, very sorry. Twenty-five years I have been here. Not possible."

My heart was deflating. "I really, really don't want to leave India, sir."

The old man grinned gently, in a way that told me he'd heard every excuse, complaint, beg, and whine from foreigners over the years. No matter how pretty, how smart, how eloquent, or how well-endowed with visa one was, he wasn't budging. "I understand. You leave India. You go on now; you go Nepal, or Bangladesh. Then you come right back!" He smiled encouragingly. I could tell he was trying to cheer me up, not to be an ass. "But must go, madame" he said, and then went back to sorting dusty files.

I'd been dismissed.

I stood there a minute, without moving. Noticing the look of despair on my face, he ended the discussion with a sympathizing head wobble. I got the feeling he'd seen more than his share of teary-eyed, bummed-out backpackers, reluctant to depart.

I mulled and muttered, pondered and pouted for a few days, sitting with the possibility of heading to Nepal for a visa run. I just wasn't *done* yet! But the bite of reality was sinking in. I was not only being kicked out of mother's nest, I was being called back to the West.

I felt the pull of my friends and family, as I caught up on months' worth of emails that had piled up while I was away from civilization. These were dear friends' loving letters—real, vibrant stories chock full of heart and soul. They described lives back home, accounts of new unions and departures, aches and pains, struggles and victories, births and deaths. I felt each message cut to my communal core. While I had felt so utterly cast adrift in the Andaman Islands, my community had never let go of the love line. No matter how far and away I was flying, I was still lightly tethered, like a cosmic kite on a string of stars…

Farewell, My Love

1st of April, Kolkata

Rest assured, sweet India, I shall return, I'll soon be back
For now, I'm moving forward, right on track
I've slept in beds of rocks, spiders and snakes
I've loved and grown so much, my heart, it aches
I can't tell you how or why it could be
Dear sweet India has such a hold on me
I love you so, my Mother, my soul
For it is here that you made me whole
And thanks to my faraway friends and tribe
I've endured every challenge, each joyful cry
Farewell, dear India, you have loved me well
A small piece of my heart remains, here to dwell

Love,
Bindi

Epilogue

I have departed from my motherland, India. A mother that brings me wave upon wave of love, and beauty. A mother that envelops me with endless compassion, courage, and creative fire. These gifts are endless.

I have bid adieu to my fellow journeyer, Jan, who wholeheartedly plunged alongside me on a grand adventure. A soul mate for a karmic season, a temporal tryst that invoked in me a wealth of wisdom, and oceans upon oceans of searing self-awareness. These gifts are timeless.

The enormity of such an experience is ineffable. Grief is a strange emotion. When we do not deny it, when we go into it fully, there are many wonders to be found while riding the wave. Suffice to say my heart is breaking. I am Broken Open.

Endless, timeless, open.

Not bad. Not bad at all. Even when it hurts like hell, it's beautiful.

Friends, this is the final chapter of our shared journey—at least in this incarnation. During the course of this journey, India has embedded enough raw material in the marrow of my bones to fill several books. Talk about grist for the mill!

I sincerely hope this journey, and all I've shared, has been of benefit to you in some significant way, whether entertaining, enlivening, or deliciously distracting. Most importantly, I pray that these writings have given you inspiration, strength, and courage to forge ahead on your own inner and outer journeys.

I dedicate this work to all beings—seen and unseen, human and non-human—who have so generously provided me with protection and strength, courage and guidance, and help along the way... even when I wasn't aware that it was all right there. There will be another journey up ahead, and I hope you join me for the next one, too.

Thank you, my friends, and thank you, Great Mystery. With a deep bow of gratitude, respect, and humility,

Namaste,
Erin Reese

Bindi Girl Travel Companion

Don't Leave Home Without It

Sure, you've read the guidebooks. But here are a few items you may not have thought about. If you're heading out for a long haul on the subcontinent, consider stuffing these in your backpack *before* you go. You won't find these easily once you're on the road, and these simple essentials will make your stay in India a whole lot more comfy. I've learned the hard way—so you won't have to.

1. Extra-strength mosquito repellent

Yes, I know it's highly toxic. But *au natural* citronella ain't gonna cut it with these buffalo-sized bloodsuckers. And India's national brand, Odomos, isn't a whole lot better than a moisturizer with an odd smell.

2. iPod or MP3 player

You'll need those homegrown mixes and tunes to keep you sane on long-haul bus and train trips. It may seem like a copout, but when things get a little sketchy, intense, or insane you'll definitely want to tune out for a while. Bring an extra set of earbuds—good quality headphones are hard to find here. My friends swear by the more costly noise-canceling varieties (which also help you endure the 24-hour plane ride).

3. Mini-speakers for iPod

Personally, these are worth their weight in gold. Nothing like putting on some music in a dowdy guest house room to clear the air and lift your spirits. My cheap, lightweight Sony speakers have survived spontaneous soirees on sandy beaches, campfires in the jungle, and dance parties in my postage-sized guest house room.

4. Bach Rescue Remedy and Rescue Sleep

These flower essence combinations are amazing, and most definitely cannot be found in India. Whether you're feeling woozy from the frenetic bus ride, wiped out from pollution and noise, or simply stressed or out-of-sorts, a shot of this homeopathic standby works absolute wonders. I keep an eyedropper bottle full in my bag at all times, and take a shot when the road is too much for my brain. Good for shock and trauma, too—or when ill to calm nerves. The new Rescue Sleep spray-on-tongue-at-bedtime formula is fantastic for an herbal rest aid.

5. Earplugs

Bring a good supply. Believe it or not, not so easily found in the backwaters. Stuff 'em in tight. India is loud. Even in the countryside, you're never alone. Some family, farm, or frenzy is going off somewhere nearby. My personal favorite are Mack's silicone earplugs, which are also great for swimming. They make an ultra-tight seal. Available at major drugstores.

6. Lightweight Sleeping Bag or sleep sack

This is a controversial item, but I feel so much happier traveling with a lightweight (down = more warmth for the weight) sleeping bag. Unless you're heading to Nepal or Kashmir in winter, usually a 15°–30° F bag is fine. It makes a huge difference—so cozy, protection from mysterious bedding, makes a great hammock liner on the beach or in the jungle (even in South India, it gets chilly pre-dawn). Overnights in second-class trains are especially chilly in the north. I love my compact down bag; it weighs only one kilo and stuffs into a small ball.

7. Headlamp or other tiny torch/flashlight

An absolute must. Carry it with you at all times. You never know when the electricity will go out in India—and it will, invariably one to three times per day. There are plenty of cow patties and other mystery objects to dodge in the road—even the random sleeping baba.

I particularly like the Petzl Zipka version, because it has a zippy stretch toggle strap that you can wear on your head (giving access to both hands), or easily snaps on to a bicycle, or worn on wrist as a bracelet light. Also comes with three different light levels (mood lighting, anyone?) as well as a flashing blinky setting in case you find yourself at a rave in Goa. It's as light as a feather, too. Whatever light you bring, make sure it takes AAA or AA batteries—the fancy high-tech lithium varieties may be hard to find on the road.

8. Combination Padlock

Remember the old-school combination lockers from high school? Bring a heavy-duty combo padlock, and commit the numbers to memory. You can use this lock in 95% of guest houses, instead of the bulky lock-and-key apparatus they'll provide.

In addition to not having to maneuver tricky skeleton keys, or risk losing a keychain with your room number and guest house boldly revealed on it, you can share the number with your travel partner so you don't have to go back and forth ("Do you have the key? When can we meet back here? Where's the key?").

Added bonus: with a luggage security chain (make yourself, purchase at home or near railway stations), you can use the padlock to secure your pack underneath the seat in the train. You'll rest much easier on overnight journeys knowing your gear is protected from quick swipes. (Although I must say, in my experience, most of India is hassle-free and I've had more theft and problems in Europe and the U.S. Yet, as they say, "Trust Allah, and tie your camel.")

9. Travel Clothesline or small length of rope.

Lewis N. Clark and a few other companies make stretchy travel clotheslines with clips on the end. You can then pick up a small pack (10-12) of plastic mini-clothespins once you're here to deter monkeys and wind gusts from nabbing your undies. The suction cups feature never works—I invariably end up throwing them away—but the toggle clips attach nicely to stretch the line between curtain and shower rods, or door handles. Even when not doing laundry, the line makes a nice apparatus for airing out items, drying sarongs, or simply to use as a place to hang clothes in the room.

10. ZIPLOC® BAGS!!!!

Bring extra. These cannot be found in India. If you can, get the fancy version with actual "zips" ("Easy Zipper" rather than standard press 'n seal variety). Due to the indomitable nature of plastic, these bags can be washed and used again and again, for six months and beyond. Use 'em to store fruit, extra biscuits, and soggy laundry, seal up mosquito repellent, or protect important documents. Get a bunch of gallon-sized ones and throw in a few sandwich-sized ones, too. You won't regret it.

Have fun, and remember the Golden Rule when packing:

When in doubt,
Leave it out...

...or you'll end up shipping four kilos of junk back home after the first week, once your back is screaming, "Why? Why?"

About the Author

Erin Reese is a one-of-a-kind explorer.

A self-described "travel and soul writer," Erin is the creator of the immensely popular spiritual-travel blog, Bindi Girl, which appeared online from 2002-2010. Her work has appeared in the business travel magazine, *Global Traveler,* featuring articles on Varanasi, Kolkata, Malaysia, and Taipei. Living a nomadic life between continents, Erin is working on her next book on India. Sign up for news, articles, and travel updates at her website, www.erinreese.com.

Bindi loves fan mail!
You can write to Bindi at:
bindigirl@gmail.com

Cheers!
— Sreekanth V

Made in the USA
Lexington, KY
19 June 2012